EPITAPH FOR THE FEW

Michael Kendrick

**An anthology of poems to commemorate the achievements
of the pilots of the Battle of Britain, 1940**

Also includes five poems written during World War Two
by **Wing Commander C. F. 'Bunny' Currant** D.S.O., D.F.C*., Croix de Guerre

Preface by **Dame Vera Lynn**

ISBN 0-9550353-1-7   978-0-9550353-1-9

Published by Michael Kendrick
© Michael Kendrick 2006

Best wishes,

Michael Kendrick

Author's **Introduction**

Michael Kendrick.

In the late spring of 1940 Great Britain was resplendent: fields rich in fresh greenery, orchards of pink and scarlet blossom, crops ripening and wild flowers pretty and profuse.

Nature's beauty, however, masked the unease of a nation on the brink of disaster, the impending possibility of a worldwide collapse in democracy, indeed the loss of civilisation's finest values!

In September 1939 fascist Germany, as a precursor towards European and planned future world domination, invaded Poland. The German Fuhrer, Adolf Hitler, and the Nazi Party held the unswerving belief that a Germanic 'super race' would rule the planet for a thousand years. Who could argue that in the Thirties, Germany possessed the world's most brilliant physicists, and they led developments into nuclear power?

The Russian despot, Josef Stalin, an equally evil man, assisted his German 'Allies' in the September 1939 invasion of Poland and shared in the victory spoils.

A May 1939 Franco-Polish pact promised the invaded country support. It was not honoured, but when Germany thrust into the Low Countries using innovative 'Blitzkrieg' tactics: storm troopers, speedy mechanised armour and close air support, a British Expeditionary Force in France was pushed back to the Channel coast. In May 1940 nearly a third of a million troops were evacuated from the French port: the miracle of Dunkirk. Our Army had

no option but to abandon most of its weaponry, while the Royal Air Force, in containing the Luftwaffe, lost one thousand aircraft, half being precious fighters. The Royal Navy offered considerable cover to the evacuation, but was extremely vulnerable to air and submarine attack, and later took shelter at Scapa Flow, Scotland.

On June 18th Winston Churchill, our prime minister said: 'The Battle of France is over; the Battle of Britain is about to begin.'

Peace terms were offered on condition that Great Britain accepted German sovereignty over Europe. On July 16th, Directive No16, code-named: 'Seelowe' (Sea Lion), was struck: 'To eliminate the English homeland as a base for the prosecution of the war against Germany.' As a prerequisite Hitler insisted: 'Provided Air superiority could be attained!'

The subsequent battle for air supremacy lasted for 114 days, from July 10th to October 31st, and Churchill described it as our 'FINEST HOUR.' Senior German officers were confident of gaining mastery of the skies, what with 3,000 aircraft at their disposal and 10,000 experienced and well-trained pilots. Initially the R.A.F. could muster 1,000 fighters and 1,500 trained pilots, many belonging to the Voluntary Reserve and University Squadrons and with little experience. Throughout the course of the battle Great Britain was defended by a spread of 2, 945 pilots, with a hard-core of around 1,000 pre-war professionals. Air Chief Marshall (later Lord) Hugh Dowding, wisely used only half of his numbers at any given time in shielding southern England.

The summer of 1940 was 'eternal', day after day the blazing sun shone as vast echelon waves of enemy aircraft droned above Kent: 'The Garden of England', and Sussex, seeking out to destroy R.A.F. aircraft and their bases. Furious 'dog-fights' developed, with civilians witnessing the heroics and sacrifices in the skies. The pressure intensified, and the young pilots in their Hurricane and Spitfire fighters either learned quickly or not at all! On the 7th September 1940 an enemy force, throughout the day 1,000 aircraft, attacked London. As usual, the air-fleet consisted of bombers protected by a phalanx of fighters. The Luftwaffe lost 60 machines, the R.A.F. just 26. On the 17th September 1940 Adolf Hitler postponed Operation 'Seelowe' indefinitely, and abandoned it completely on October 10th.

Winston Churchill, in his magnificent and historic speech said: "Never in the field of human conflict was so much owed by so many to so Few." The Few lost 544 pilots in the battle and a further 795 did not survive the war.

The air victory was of pivotal importance regarding the outcome of the Second World War. Not only was it mighty Germany's first defeat, but also it lifted the moral of our nation, and eventually

led Hitler to turn his attention towards the U.S.S.R. With a war on two fronts the eventual outcome was obvious, and ultimately it was the U.S.A. who delivered the first neutron chain reaction.

The poems reflect my deep feelings of respect and gratitude to a brotherhood of magnificent men, we shall never see their likes again...

My most sincere gratitude to Martin Bird for the brilliant graphic design work.

FRONT COVER: The front cover comes from a painting by Geoffrey Nutkins: 'Despatching Franz von Werra.' It depicts Squadron Leader Gerald Stapleton of 603 Squadron shortly after shooting down the enemy pilot, later famed in the film: 'The One That Got Away.' The scene is Love's Farm, near Marden, Kent, on the 5th September 1940.

My sincere gratitude to Geoff, undoubtedly a world-class aviation artist. He and his dear wife, Lesley, have been great friends for many years. Together they have done and continue to do so much for the Few. www.aviartnutkins.com

Squadron Leader Gerald Stapleton

Preface

Dame Vera Lynn.

I have been aware of Michael's devotion to the 'Few', those wonderfully brave pilots who defended our skies throughout the 1940 Battle of Britain, for many years now. Often I have congratulated him on his great talent with words, and I know that his friends within the 'Few' appreciate his efforts and abilities. One gentleman in particular, Wing Commander 'Bunny' Currant often praises Michael's contribution to ensuring the eternal memory of the sacrifices of 1940 and beyond. The late Group Captain Dennis David adored his output so much so that he hailed Michael as: 'The Battle of Britain Poet'.

Michael modestly says that the quality within the poetry simply reflects the eminence and bravery of his friends, and certainly his heartfelt feelings stand out for all to read. I applaud his efforts, and feel his poems will abide for a long time within the hearts of readers, as well as archival records. It is so contenting to know that such verse captures the heroics of those young men in their Hurricanes and Spitfires.

Sincerely Yours,

Vera Lynn

Dame Vera Lynn. June 2005.

Dedicated to **Wing Commander C.F. 'Bunny' Currant**

D.S.O., D.F.C.*, Croix de Guerre, Mentioned in Despatches*.

A scene showing Bunny in the wartime film; 'The First of The Few.'

As a teenager in the late 1950s I read many a thrilling biography concerning Battle of Britain pilots. They included Douglas Bader's: 'Reach for the Sky', Bob Stanford Tuck's: 'Fly For Your Life' and 'Wing Leader' regarding Leicestershire's very own 'Johnnie' Johnson. Such sacrifice and heroism inspired me. To read about the 'Brotherhood of the Few', to watch films capturing the spirit of the R.A.F., and to hear recordings of Winston Churchill's dramatic and inspiring speeches, made me appreciate that our freedom came at a price!

During my middle years I was fortunate indeed to be befriended by many of my heroes, and as they 'thin-out' with the passage of time I will never, ever, forget them. Undoubtedly I am a finer person for having shared a part of their lives; perhaps stardust has sprinkled onto my undeserving shoulders, and where, I ask, are today's role models?

A relative, Arthur Newberry Choyce was Leicestershire's Great War poet, and having written poetry since the early 1960s, I considered only a Poet Laureate worthy of writing about the exploits of the Few.

Bunny and I have been grand friends for over two decades, he has a love of poetry, and he asked me to forward one or two of my 'nature themes'. From then he was a constant source of encouragement, and without that this anthology would never have been written. If readers consider the verse acceptable then please understand that men of high quality inspired it to be so.

Christopher Frederick Currant joined the R.A.F. as a direct entry pilot in 1936. The following year he began with 46 Squadron and joined 151 Squadron at North Weald in 1939.

Bunny served with 605 Squadron throughout the Battle and was one of the foremost ace pilots, receiving a D.F.C. on 8th October 1940, a Bar on 15th November 1940, and the D.S.O. on 7th July 1942. He was also awarded a Belgium Croix de Guerre and was twice 'mentioned in despatches'. Following a spell at an Officer Training Unit he took command of 501 Squadron at Ibsley, and from 15th February 1943 until July 1944 led the Ibsley Wing.

A graduate of the Joint Services Staff College and the Royal Air Force College, he served in British Intelligence after the war at the White House in the U.S.A. as well as a similar post in Norway. He was to receive the equivalent of our knighthood from the King of that country for his outstanding services.

"The only thing necessary for the triumph of evil is for good men to do nothing."

(Philosopher Edmund Burke.)

Contents

Opposite: A black and white version of Geoff Nutkin's coloured painting: 'Spitfire Over Kent Hopfields'. Wing Commander Bob Doe of 234 Squadron flying over hopfield workers in Kent during the summer of 1940.

A Fall To Grace

Kent 1940

'A deathly plume, a black cloak of oily smoke."

We spin through space in ever closing circles,
Engine and fabric consumed by a blazing mesh.
A deathly plume, a black cloak of oily smoke:
A grim mourner, mingling at a burial pyre.
I missed my assailant in a blinding sun,
And the error gnaws grimly at my soul.

At last I eject from a cockpit of fierce flames,
With bliss to be corrupted by utter despair.
My chute singed as wings of a candle-lit moth,
And gravity is drawing me to an earthly grave.
Down through a spiralling stairway of smoke,
And far below, the eye of my Hurricane.

The aircraft's wreck a portent of my death,
Air-currents wither the flesh on cheekbones.
Ears thump to the drumbeats of a distant battle,
I jettison my charred and crisped parachute.
Nostrils are smoke-blasted: throat tightens,
Cannot swallow: it's locked and ragingly sore.

So this is my fate: what life has held in store,
It's not a nightmare: yet soon I will sleep more.
The rushing earth resembles a boy's bed-quilt,
"Get up Michael you'll be late for school!"
I'd lost conscious and was dreaming of home,
There's so much more I need to do with my life!

I feel weightless and wish this to be the case,
Maybe a tree or haystack will break my descent.
Oh, please God help me to survive this fall,
If only for the promise I made to my wife.
"Congratulation upon your wonderful wedding,
May you have many happy years together."

It's so dreadfully cold and I can't stop shaking,
A patchwork of farmland soon to be awakened.
Thoughts are racing-away through my mind,
And so many plans waste-away into the ether.
"Are you sure you want to join the R.A.F?
Your father says you'd be safer in the Army".

Earth has lost curvature: clouds their mystery,
I fall at speed towards an unblessed cemetery.
'Yes sir, I will lookout for the 'Hun in the Sun',
Said I regarding comments taken as obvious.
"Jump in the back, we're off to the White Hart,
You shot two down today so it's your round."

Hurry, at long last, it will soon be over with,
Now for reality, or an end, only seconds to live!
I see a pinkie-hue, the blossom of orchard trees,
That song: 'I'll be with you in apple blossom time.'
"Wrap up warm, I don't want you absent
  from school.
Please mother, don't fuss I can look after myself."

"I'll be with you in apple blossom time,
I'll be with you to change your name to mine."
Michael's body was found cradled in the branches
  of a fruit tree.
It was partially concealed by a heavy sprinkling
  of apple blossom.
A military headstone marks the spot where he had
  a fall to grace.

**Let this poem be dedicated to all airmen who
met the same fate.**

*"The aircraft's wreck a
portent of my death."*

Dedicated to **Wing Commander T.F. Neil**
D.F.C.*, A.F.C., A.E.

Tom and his dear wife and ex W.A.A.F. Eileen, 2005.

Tom in 1940.

A Fighter In My Sights

Born at the mouth of the Mersey, uncalled as
  a sea-faring man,
No salty veins, only flying adventures and
  a thirst for wingspan.
Memories of Old Dock Road and steamy
  Lime Street Station,
Memories of a move to Manchester: little joy
  or expectation.

Oh to be a Liver Bird and ascend into a
  shimmering haze,
Oh for the valiant pilots that emerged during
  pre-war days.
Tall Tom, a dashing pilot with Squadron two-
  four-nine,
'Gold Coast', a nationally recognised emblem
  and top line.

Church Fenton and Leconsfield; what a daring
  flight at night:
It was of total darkness, only befitted a blind
  man's sight.
Perhaps searchlights, dead men's fingers,
  lit the unique course,
And helped 'Ginger' to locate base by
  some unnatural force.

A stunning sun concealed bandits in battles of
  life and death,
With Tom sharp of mind and reflex plus lots
  of bated breath.
Gun button to fire and shredded swastika wings
  over southern town,
To be followed by trials and tribulations at
  Boscombe Down.

September at North Weald amid scrambles and
  lots of tally-ho,
Bearing witness to lethal dogfights upon
  confronting the foe.
Hurricane 'G.N.F.' shrieked into attacks at
  2850 revolutions,
With Tom Neil D. F. C. and bar well worthy of
  his decorations.

Dear pals: Pat Wells, John Grandy, Butch, and
  John Beazley,
Ozzie, 'Tommy' Thompson, Bentley Beard and
  George Barclay.
'Nick' Nicholson's bravery a cameo of that ventured
  by the Few,
And merited with highest award of the Victoria
  Cross too.

Christmas Day of 1940 and Tom twenty and
  five months old,
Not in his dreams thought that one-day his story
  would be told.
Lunch with Bader, 'Sailor' Malan and company,
  a junior son,
While Leigh Mallory stated: 'The Battle of Britain
  was won!'

Set in the Mediterranean Sea: a jewel of an isle
  we call Malta,
Our pilots besieged but at no time did
  two-four-nine falter.
Oh to be a Liver Bird and ascend into a
  shimmering haze,
Tom displayed great skill and bravery during
  his R.A.F. days.

Winston Churchill named that rare and gifted breed:
  The Few,
Possessed a spirit and resilience that an enemy
  failed to undo.
Memories of a Merseyside lad during Battle of
  Britain fights,
Can be read within the pages of: 'A Fighter in
  my Sights'.* * Tom's autobiography.

Searchlights: 'dead men's fingers'.

In memory of **Pilot Officer I.J. 'Jock' Muirhead**

D.F.C., a dear friend of Wing Commander C.F. 'Bunny' Currant.

I.J. 'Jock' Muirhead

A Lion with Wings

Clouds of cirrus, cumulus or nimbus with their
  kaleidoscopic ways,
Arranged within a blue heaven in the late Thirties
  of pre-war days.
Two young pilots with solar haloes and roundel
  markings on aircraft,
Diving in gamely Gloster Gauntlets and soaring
  thanks to a rotary shaft.

Enter 1939 and World War 2 with cities subject
  to enemy bombing,
And black tear-laden clouds relate to the dead
  and pitiful sobbing.
Two young pilots with names of Jock and
  Bunny with 605 Squadron,
Flying with the Brotherhood of the Few to defy
  the Devil's cauldron.

The 22nd April 1940 and Bunny crash-landed
  near to Arras in France,
Four days on and Jock was shot-down patrolling
  the Dunkirk stance.
Our tall Scot evaded capture and departed by
  cargo-ship from Ostend,
To see machine-guns kill friends: from life to
  death as spirits ascend.

The two stalwarts toughened the defences of
  England's northeast,
And the unescorted bombers of Luflotte 5 proved
  something of a feast.
Jock was the Squadron's first to receive the
  Distinguished Flying Cross,
A mercurial ace pilot who achieved eventual
  victory at Germany's loss.

A 7th August flight to Croydon and descent
  onto a bombed-out Station,
And scramble with Archie and the lads to rip
  into an enemy formation.
From Angels 20 came waves of enemy fighters
  and down went Yellow 3,
Down, down in flames, one more youthful
  sacrifice for our country.

The 7th October and Jock torched a 109 fighter
  with a four second burst,
Only to recoil with rudder damage from a
  wingman of similar thirst.
Downwards went Hurricane V 7305 out of
  control and in a sickly spin,
And to Bunny's relief a figure appeared and
  jumped-out from within.

Jock warmly applauded Bunny's D.F.C. and
  a bar for Archie McKellar,
As all of 605 were impressed by the dynamic
  wee Glaswegian fella.
Autumn's leaves turned to a scarlet red and
  finally yellow gold,
And soon another of the Few was to perish and
  join a heavenly fold.

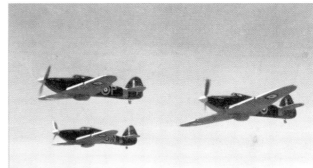

October 15th and Jock was flying N2546 for an
  interception over Kent,
As a swarm of fighters dived with guns blazing
  and fully hell-bent.
*"Jock died a man doing his duty fearlessly
  and bravely"*
"He was a Lion with Wings", said Bunny solemnly.

Jock Muirhead on the left, enjoys a drink with friends, 1940.

Dedicated to the memory of **Pilot Officer K.R. Gillman**
R.A.F. Hawkinge

Keith Gillman is sitting second from the right. Rupert Smythe had discarded his two pages (to his right).

A Moment In Time

A serene scene, a time of war, the click of lens,
 a print of the past.
The figures whole: the sun was high, a camera true,
 no shadows cast.
Seven young men apparently at ease, maybe
 awaiting another sortie.
A moment in time at Hawkinge, pilots of
 32 Squadron in July 1940.

Smart blue uniforms, chunky Mae Wests and
 silvery wings on show.
Five men squatting, heads at 12 o'clock high
 while others lay low.
Some have cheery faces while some a degree
 of contemplation.
Rupert read two pages only to discard them
 without explanation.

Keith's face so recognisable, eternally young,
 never changing.
Innocence of teenage eyes, vivid yet naïve,
 virtuous and engaging.
Life was short, his days not long, now he sleeps
 on a Channel bed.
Six survived the war, the toss of a dice,
 they had happiness instead.

Pilots of the Few, they fought to secure our
 freedom against iniquity.
Young men too, they defied all to ensure our way
 of life with victory.
The Hurricane in the scene became a casualty:
 didn't remain on view.
The flying craft was soon to exchange a field
 of green for a sea of blue.

In 2000 I strolled from Hawkinge Museum to
 the 1940 picture spot.
The noonday sun's rays were dazzling and my
 imagination was hot.
Did I see seven faces squatting and looking at me,
 there on the green?
The nearby houses appear to be wholly unchanged,
 sentinel and serene.

Keith was reported missing on the 25th August 1940.

Blackwell Wood

Kent 2001

I scaled the chalky incline to explore the ancient
  wood of Brenchley.
A canopied and carpeted refuge scarcely visited
  for over a century.
Upon arrival a steamy sun greeted me, though
  dappled by the trees.
An awakening daybreak mist had bathed,
  bathed the flighty leaves.

Two fox cubs shared a peep and stole off,
  one had a snowy tipped tail.
A legion of slimy Roman snails slid-on,
  leaving a glistening trail.
Ageing oaks, elms and ash cradled with ivy that
  clung for all it was worth.
A squirrel at feast, carrion crows and a nesting
  thrush waiting birth.

A sudden clearance in the thickly thatched wood,
  unnaturally clear.
Skeletal sets of trunks and bluebells and fungi
  sprouted here and there.
A dark pond hid a deep sorrow: an earthly scar
  wept into a streamlet.
A moss green and bone-grey headstone: words
  I will never forget.

The unrestricted sun eased the nape of my neck,
  a comfort to me.
Nearer to the stone the epitaphic lines became clear,
  clearer to see.
'Somewhere beneath this isolated spot rests
  teenage Pilot Officer Y.'
'One of the Few and we live because by his
  bravery he was to die'.

Eyes of sadness and pride pictured the events
  that happened there.
The sun became totally eclipsed as angry storm
  clouds spread fear.
No lightning only the crash of a thunderbolt
  from directly above.
An eerie light and a Spitfire flew over with the
  silence of a dove.

Richard Hope Hillary.

An Eternal Victory

A young man patently among the finest
  and brightest of his generation.
Whatever indulged he invariably succeeded
  and with great distinction.
The virtues of boarding school and thereafter
  degree studies at Oxford.
A tall and fine athlete with a winning desire
  even at the cost of blood.

He was all these and a sprinkle of arrogance,
  a product of his class.
Well-liked by friends but to others could appear
  aloof, but never crass.
 By disposition was equipped to lead from the
  front and desired to do so.
All of the requirements for success and a charm
  that friends got to know.

A daring member of the University Squadron,
  it was all an adventure.
No notion of killing or being so entered training
  by any such measure.
He enjoyed solo high flights and a singular
  control to forge a destiny.
In 1940 an ace pilot with 603 Squadron and he
  flew in good company.

Richard bailed-out of his blazing aircraft,
  it pierced a foaming sea.
Hospital life as one of McIndoe's 'Guinea Pigs'
  and yearned to be free.
Months of suffering from fire-charred face and
  hands: devastating pain.
Skin grafts with brine-baths, and loss of liberty:
  nearly drove him insane.

Tens of squadron and university friends perished
  in a naked sky so blue.
A feeling part of his soul had died with the
  passing of friends in the Few.
Physically and mentally scarred he wished that
  in battle he'd been killed.
An intense belief that all was lost and dreams
  were never to be fulfilled.

He sought refuge in private solace whether from
  friends or strangers.
Childhood demons and insecurities resurrected
  themselves to pose dangers.
Nothing in life was clear, only a deep anger:
  and failure to direct his rage.
A belief that if he could redeem himself he'd
  turn over life's next page.

Perhaps he had a masterly plan: appearing to renew
his strength and dignity.
He reclaimed his wings as a night fighter; was life
pointing towards reality?
Seemingly Richard regained his aura of authority
and with it a status to fly.
Whilst piloting a Blenheim it crashed and by total
cremation was to die.

'The Last Enemy': now an Eternal Victory.

The Last Enemy was first published in June 1942.

Recovering from burns, 1942.

The first committee of the Guinea Pig Club. From left: Tom Gleave, Geoffrey Page, Russell Davies,
Peter Weeks, John Hughes, Michael Coote and Archibald McIndoe (Surgeon).
Photo: Thanks to Geoffery Page.

In memory of **Group Captain Sir Douglas Bader** 1910 - 1982
K.B.E., D.S.O.*, D.F.C.*, Legion d'Honneur, Croix de Guerre, Mentioned in Despatches.***

Douglas Bader on the cockpit of his Hurricane. (With thanks to the Bader Foundation).

Bader

Tough, strong, decisive, brave and commanding.
Pertinent, forthright, supportive, confident
  and demanding.
The name preceded the man: the man maketh
  the name!
We will never see Bader's like on this earth
  ever again.

Forget forms of triplicate: only time to file them
  in the bin.
So direct with a hustle and bustle: a potent
  spirit within.
Stubby pipe, tricky undercarriage, big eyes
  and a square jaw.
Limits, boundaries, soft pedal. Never, once
  he'd set the score!

Thrusting gait driven by athletic and dynamic
  muscular thighs.
Piloting was no problem when so gifted in
  unchaining earthly ties.
A metallic pair of legs took poll spot when
  he led his squadrons.
Bader's Big Wings spread terror into invading
  aerial formations.

Johnnie Johnson, Hugh Dundas, Al Smith:
  a Legion d'Honneur.
Dear Douglas always at the front, a knight in
  shining armour.
It's true he wore a blunt façade but it concealed
  a heart of gold.
It was he who assisted the disabled and helped
  them to be bold.

An inspirational character, a trusted, trusting
  and sincere man.
Hated falseness, detested deceit, a master at
  exposing all sham.
His charitable care, kindness and strength
  benefited mankind.
As other great men he has his memory
  occasionally maligned.

Where now is Douglas, where can that legendary
  spirit be found?
Doubtless gracing the heavens, flying in a
  Spitfire I'll be bound.
Remember the name; remember the man,
  a model for us all.
He was the flyer with tin legs, but for me he
  always stood tall.

Douglas Bader with (Sir) Alan Smith.

Douglas Bader entertains the Queen Mother.

A tribute to **Group Captain Sir Douglas Bader**

Douglas receives an honorary degree from Calgary University. His wife, Betty, accompanies him.
Photo: With thanks to Betty Bader.

Bader Too

With his deep orbital eyes, obedient wiry hair
  and rugged jaw.
A sharply positive mind, a man of stamina
  and potency galore.
Engaging of stance, props and dynamic frame:
  sinewy thighs.
Source of stimulation, fear not of failure,
  just reach for the skies.

A formidable figure and character: always
  truthful and direct.
Visited the sick and disabled: vowed to improve
  and protect.
Belief flowed as a mountain stream, never
  subject to whim.
Bader's confidence and faith invigorated folks
  around him.

A leader of men whether on terra firma or in
  high atmosphere.
Rare is the man of such strength and resource
  to combat fear.
I picture a golden Spitfire initialled D.B. in the
  heavenly blue.
The aircraft markings are familiar and the
  pilot's face is too.

In memory of **Wing Commander A.G. Page** 1920 - 2000

OBE., D.S.O.*, D.F.C.*

Geoffrey Page.

Capel Le Ferne

Revisited 2002

Geoffrey's dream fulfilled at Capel, a meditative
 and memorial spot.
The Few knew 'Hell's Corner', in 1940 the
 action was tragically hot.
It sits upon steep white cliffs where Vera Lynn's
 blue birds fly high.
A worthy sculpture and shrine to the Few
 who met death in the sky.

Pilgrims will continue to revere the names
 listed upon yon heights.
They'll recall the sacrifice of young braves
 amid dogged aerial fights.
A chalky and lofty locale with greenery and
 'tis nearer to heaven too!
Once their sweethearts waited at a time when
life was joyful and new.

God watch over 'Friends of the Few' at
 Geoffrey's chosen sanctuary.
Remember that in the Battle of Britain they
 secured a notable victory.
So, blow freely you salty Channel air and soothe
 both mind and spirit.
They were to the right-of-the-line and history
 records with due merit.

(With thanks to the Museum and to Geoffrey for
his photographs)

Memorial at Capel Le Ferne.

Throughout boyhood, Roly's pocket money was hoarded to buy flying books and materials for making aeroplane models. With thanks to Roly for photograph.

Boyhood Dreams Fulfilled

Hometown Chichester with cathedral spire,
   harbour and South Downs.
A range of flora, fauna, and man-made mechanical
   airborne sounds.
R.A.F. Tangmere a local magnet to attract boys
   with its aero tricks,
With biplanes diving, soaring and creating a
   stunning mix.
Six-years-old Roly in an Avro 504 for a baptism
   and a flying start.
Youthful training in a Tiger Moth completely stole
   his heart.

In the R.A.F. and grades are rewarded with a
   commission and wings.
World War 2 arrives together with the extra
   responsibly that brings.
A bleakly cold Phoney War then combats blight
   spring's fragrance,
As Roly fights with 87 Squadron during the 1940
   Battle of France.
'United Provinces' score over eighty victories
   in ten days of May.
Nine airmen 'bought it' by giving their tomorrows
   for our today.

Exeter base, farewell Flanders' lace, enemy attack
   in huge forces.
Fierce fights, summer heights, over-stretched by
   minimal resources.
Swastikas and smoke-trails over a Solent blasted
   by reverberations,
As all pilots strained in the searing heat of
   dogfights and tribulations!
The impact of collisions for friend and foe in a
   crowded sky.
Then all alone except the reassuring cooling
   clouds close by.

Roly, one of a brotherly band whose names
   will live for evermore.
Charmy Down, a full squadron posting with
   night action being in store.
Silvery moonlight, stars-a-twinkle and ghostly
   reflections in cloud,
And 'Gdumphy' at control, owl-wise advice
   conveyed clear and loud.
He often repeated on transmission that he didn't
   really give a hoot.
*"It doesn't concern whether you return by
   aeroplane or parachute!"*

Kent and R.A.F. Manston flying Typhoons as
  'C.O.' of Squadron 609.
Long wintry patrols over an ice-cold Channel
  in visibility far from fine.
Jugs of beer at the Old Charles pub and a
  roaring post horn fanfare,
The Nook and Cherry Brandy pub with memories
  and sausages to share.
Roly's Typhoon 'PR-G' active by night, often lit
  by a waxing moon.
Steely rails and smoky sparks all attracted his
  train-busting boom.

Not a Shakespearean Fantasy but a new fighter-
  bomber, the Tempest.
A Wing Commander with D.S.O. and D.F.C.
  never gave the Hun a rest.
450 miles-per-hour at only fifteen feet to destroy
  Cormeille's aerodrome,
And 'Kelvin Leader' was satisfied and rapidly
  set a course for home.
Led a Wing of raging Tempests over Normandy's
  beaches on 'D'-Day.
Personally destroyed 32 'doodlebugs' with a nudge
  from a wing sway.

Still deeper into Holland with a five squadron
  Tempest Wing at Volkel.
Daily combat with enemy fighters including
  Hitler's latest jets from hell.
On the 12th October '44 over Arnhem and
  strafing an armed troop train,
Roly is hit by fierce flak so allowing his radiator
  coolant to fall like rain!
Crash-landing and arrest by a German corporal:
  "For you the war is over".
An enforced absence from folks in Chichester
  and the white cliffs of Dover.

Repatriation and success followed as a Test Pilot
  on the prototype Canberra.
Three record crossings of the Atlantic recorded by
  a television camera.
He never forgot the Lightning fighter labelled as
  the TSR2,
And eventually was appointed a director of
  English Electric too.
Six-years-old Roly in an Avro 504 for a baptism
  and a flying start.
Youthful training in a Tiger Moth completely
  stole his heart.

Roly's Hurricane.

(Roly was a lifelong friend of Dennis David)

In memory of **Group Captain Dennis David** 1918 - 2000
C.B.E., D.F.C.*, Freeman of the City of London.

Dennis 'Hurricane' David.

Dennis 'Hurricane' David

87 Squadron's legendary pilot of World War 2
  in the Hawker Hurricane.
A unique and matchless pairing of man and
  machine in perfect unison.
The 1940 blitzkrieg as the Luftwaffe bombed
  towns and cities in France.
Dennis and his pals registered enemy kills to
  show a defiant stance.
Fearful battles in May whilst facing huge odds:
  life's a toss of the dice.
Crippling losses as our pilots 'bought it':
  they paid the ultimate price.
Perhaps Agincourt archers with arrows of
  perfect flight pointed the way.
A Dunkirk evacuation to our motherland for
  troops to fight another day.

British Lion ensnared by the jawed outline of
  the European continent.
German wolves and eagles with incisors and
  talons bearing evil intent.
A thousand years of self-rule and even a mighty
  French emperor failed.

Only our R.A.F. Fighter Command could ensure
  our freedom prevailed.
Dennis knew it was a battle that had to be won:
  no matter what the cost!
Time and again we relied on heroic pilots:
  of which many were to be lost.

The pivotal Battle of Britain and Churchill's Few
  set the pace.
'Hurricane' David a battle experienced leader
  and fighter ace.
Master of eight machine-guns that ripped, rattled
  and a final recoil.
A Junkers 88 downed by Dennis whilst avoiding
  a Messerschmitt foil.
The Hardest Day, August 18th, a melting pot
  to decide our nation's life.
A momentous battle involving white heat, death,
  struggle and strife.

A German defeat despite a huge numeric
  superiority and deployment.
They continued in sinister skies in the manner of
  a night blitz movement.
The blessed Few saved lives and won our freedom,
  remember Cats' Eyes?
Nazi plan of invading our island was finally kaput:
  never to materialise.
Next, Fighter Command's eyes turned to the
  'Land of the rising sun'.
For Dennis, another theatre of war and a far-eastern
  battle to be won.

1943 at Ceylon with Dennis in 89 Squadron as
  a wing commander.
Then as a senior controller at Trincomalee and
  base at Mineriya.
1944 promotion to Group Captain and advisor to
  the 15th India Corpse.
Successful liberation of Burma and dear old
  Raffles at Singapore.
Honorary Aide to Viscount Trenchard and Air
  Attaché' in Budapest.
An amazingly brave 'pimpernel' in Hungary
  during the 1956 unrest.

Hurricanes of 87 Squadron.

Dennis at Elvington, near York, 1997.

Tally ho, dear friend: often in our thoughts.

(Dennis and Roly Beamont were lifelong friends.
With thanks to Margaret David)

Dispersal

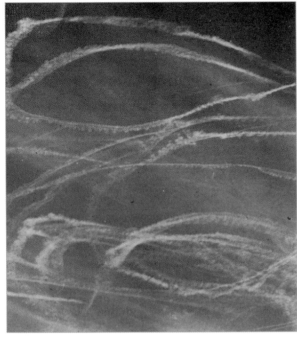

Contrails reveal dogfights in the heavens over Kent in 1940.

July was maturing and the sun-blessed hours
 were seemingly endless.
A few flyers matured while innocent chicks
 were only once guileless.
The powdery blue heavens of 1940 with their
 wispy-white contrails,
Where history recorded an air battle over
 Canterbury Pilgrims' trails.

The silent grass airfield welcomed a weary
 flight of aquiline Spitfires.
They circled before downing to a cushioned bump
 as earth met tyres.
Youthful pilots climbed from cockpits to slide
 down elliptical wings,
To renew affiliation with terra firma and find
 what the morrow brings.

Within the dusty and oily Dispersal hut are
 trophies, kills of the Few.
Four lads sat around a table with piles of change
 and a deck of cards too.
Ken read about cars and Michael played
 his gramophone by the door,
Whereas most dozed or arrowed the dartboard with
 a regular score.

Dennis was scribbling a letter while John
 was drained and slept it out.
Bunny enjoyed a relaxing pipe smoke and
 quite oblivious to all about.
Pete examined a section of enemy wing in which
 he claimed half share,
And then fell into a deep sleep with legs
 straddled across a rickety chair.

Three sat on an old sofa boisterously reliving
 their part in the last sortie.
Teddy was skimming a newspaper while lying
 next to his dog, Scottie.
A flight lieutenant was solemn and sat alone,
 his pal had just 'bought it',
When suddenly a phone rang: near sending
 a sleeping orderly into a fit.

The klaxon outside the hut sprang into life
 and a scramble, scramble.
Mitchell's marvels roared along the runway
 with little time to preamble.
From a swift burst of energetic fury Dispersal
 dulled into non-activity,
And a flight of Spitfires vectored at angels
 fifteen quite deliberately.

Within the dusty and oily Dispersal hut are trophies,
  kills of the Few.
A single dart had missed the board whilst others
  had totalled only 22.
A mixture of men and armour like knights of old
  on spirited steeds,
And fleece-lined boots that perish into flames
  during heroic deeds.

Playing cards were scattered while aces and
  gaming change had flown.
King was now high and the bearer's schemes
  would never be known.
Pilots were climbing sky-high as a web trapped
  a fly on a windowsill,
And Michael's wind-up turntable would forever
  be soundless and still.

Dennis, John and car mad Ken came home
  with success to their name.
Pete's Spitfire was bounced by two 109s
  and exploded into a ball of flame.
Dear old Bunny continued to puff his briar pipe
  and encouraged all,
And Scottie the dog vanished when Teddy was
  last seen in free-fall.

Just two of the three boisterous lads returned to
  the wide-berth sofa.
The other space remained empty to the memory
  of a pilot-brother.
The lieutenant was wearily pleased to have
  survived another scramble,
And prayed that any fallen chicks died quickly
  and not in a fiery gamble.

Within the dusty and oily Dispersal hut are trophies, kills of the Few.

Dreamy Depths of Reality

Summer 1940

The Spitfire plunged into the sea.

The Spitfire's arc sliced a pathway through
  the innocent skyline.
Scars of orange-red flame and black smoke
  in summer sunshine.
An injured pilot and a glowing-hot machine
  plunged into the sea.
Was he to escape or accept the inevitability of
  death for victory?

The craft dived into the blue: a weighty discharge
  from the sky.
Above was effervescent foam: below a scalding
  oily bath to fry.
The pilot regained consciousness on the dark
  and murky bed.
Alone and trapped within his cockpit thinking of
  the day he wed.

Upon his burnt face and hands a gradual trickle
  of cooling silt.
He thought of his wife and family and the first
  time he wore a kilt.
After a minute passed or maybe an hour's sleep
  on a Channel bed!
A shuddered wake from a dream amid thoughts
  of death by lead.

The noble sun watched from twelve o'clock in
  that 1940 sky.
Scores of gladiatorial pilots in an orbital arena
  and lots would die!
The pastel blue of the heavens: the chalky white
  of the cirrus.
Death in foamy-white crests: life in dreams only
  to deceive us.

The enemy 109 fighters swooped down from
  twenty thousand feet.
The Spitfire ace had no chance even though he
  was one of the elite.
The pilot attempted to bank to his left and depart
  his dying machine.
Trapped in his cockpit he and aircraft were
  swallowed by the brine.

Elegy to Keith Gillman

December 16th 1920 - August 25th 1940. Pilot Officer. 32 Squadron. Battle of Britain.

Keith Gillman.

Too young to register a political vote,
Too young to drive on national highways.
Old enough to fly an aircraft in skyways,
Old enough to die in a Channel moat!

He loved old Kent with her white Downs,
He loved Dover home and where he schooled.
Had the willpower to fly that never cooled,
Had the chance to be a pilot with no bounds.

The beginning of the Second World War,
The beginning of a teenage dream came true.
With wings and a uniform of airforce blue,
With wings for flights and logs to keep score.

The sun drenched twenty-fifth of August,
The sun drenched Hawkinge a radiant treat.
Keith saw white cliffs at ten thousand feet,
Keith saw fields of oats and barley husk.

Lots of orbital hazy-blue on the skyline,
Lots of palatial clouds that rose to heaven.
A Channel blue, a Me109 that struck at seven,
A Channel bed, of life there was not a sign.

He was a handsome boy and one of the Few,
He was nineteen years and soon to come of age.
His photo is preserved for ever on this page,
His photo appeared on recruitment posters too.

Keith's is remembered on the Runnymede Memorial, Panel 8.

Messerschmitt Bf 109.

Epitaph for The Few

Remembering the Summer of 1940

Was it the charted destiny of our planet or purely
  a matter of fate?
Could it be that at twenty thousand feet heavenly
  souls cumulate?
Shrouded by clouds, sparkling droplets of
  holy water,
Some young flyers were like lambs to the slaughter!
Not tear-laden clouds, but forever white and
  misty cool,
Allay the memory of pilots consumed by
  burning fuel.
Eddies that swirl and whirl strands from a
  holy edifice,
Reminiscent of a miraculous spider spinning
  at bliss.
Unclipped wings rank high on aviators' whims,
And come sunset, our earthborn stars flicker
  as twilight dims.
The twinkling of an eye, dawn, and the expectancy
  it will bring,

A gift of life and love from our creative King.
Oh such grandeur, the numinous colours of the sun,
God's light on misty water, a particularly vivid
  rainbow for the chosen!
They say the 'few' were just ordinary young men,
  brave and true!
How extraordinary that over five hundred died
  for folk such as you.
They fly high with the wings of angels, and we
  must always remember
To commemorate the Battle of Britain on the
  15th day of September.

In memory of **Squadron Leader J.H. Lacey** 1917 - 1989
D.F.M.*, Croix de Guerre, Mentioned in Despatches.

One of the Few, 1940.

Ginger

A pensive and taciturn character from Wetherby
   town in good old Yorkshire.
Grammar school led to chemist dispensing but
   flight his only chosen career.
A 1937 R.A.F.V.R. and called-up at the birth of
   the Second World War.
With 501 Squadron in the springtime Battle of
   France as a sergeant-pilot star.

During two weeks he was bombed and almost
   drowned in a swamp out there.
The French recognised his qualities and awarded
   him a Croix de Guerre.
The summer of 1940 and a focussed Ginger got
   stuck-in and showed his metal.
A leading ace fighter pilot who was awarded the
   Distinguished Flying Medal.

Buckingham Palace was bombed on 13th
   September by a Heinkel one-one-one.
Lacey's vengeful guns smashed it to earth for
   another battle won-won-won.
Ginger the flying genius disposed of
   Messerschmitts, Dorniers and Heinkels.
Something of a rebel but no one could argue with
   a pilot with twenty-plus kills!

A dedicated fighter flyer that when shot down
   would always bounce back.
Pilot officer in '41 and added promotion to flight
   lieutenant kept him on track.
His tactics for air-combat merited a position of
   chief at No1 Attack School.
In India and trained Squadron 20 'Lysander men'
   to a Hurricane fighter pool.

Ginger had similar ventures with units against
   the Japanese in the Far East.
However it was Europe where he plundered his
   bountiful and favoured feast.
Ginger served with great distinction and he will
   remain an ace amongst aces.
An odd character but again a winner when
   spending a day at Wetherby races.

A tribute to **Wing Commander G.C. Unwin**

D.S.O., D.F.M.*

George Unwin.

Grumpy

Born in Bolton-on-Dearne, a proud Yorkshire man
 to the core.
Made of northern grit, steely Sheffield just over
 yon fields for sure.
With brains and ambition he joined the R.A.F. as
 a young clerk.
Set his heart on learning to fly as superbly as the
 morning lark.

Success and he joined 19 Squadron as a fledgling
 Sergeant Pilot.
A fine aviator and became a true expert with the
 deflection shot.
One of the first to privilege piloting the aquiline
 Spitfire was George.
A lucrative liaison with enemy aircraft served as
 a feast to gorge.

A display of bravery and concern as engine failure
 forced a landing.
Risked his all in a crash to avoid children in a field
 that were playing!
The perils of war and a squadron move to
 Hornchurch to see a miracle.
Dunkirk: thanks to the Navy and the R.A.F. for
 preventing a debacle.

George and Douglas Bader were old pals: and
 amity was not skin-deep.
Bader commenced repairs to 'legs' whilst weary
 George was fast asleep.
Words said and Bader referred to a character in
 the film: 'Snow White'.
Shut-up-'Grumpy' and the name stuck but the
 terminology far from right.

The Battle of Britain and George one of the
 Few with other ace names.
A truly heroic figure that featured in many
 schoolboy's victory dreams.
He often flew in Doug Bader's 'Big Wing':
 driving the Luftwaffe insane.
A proficient pilot and a confidant of the great
 fellow tyke, 'Sandy' Lane.

Grumpy happily received a worthy commission
 in the late summer of 1941.
A 613 Squadron pilot who took to the wooden
 Mosquito like a hole-in-one.
Post-war operations in Iraq and Singapore finally
 completed a tour de force.
But pal, George, is never happier than when teeing
 on Ferdown's golf course.

I dream that I revisit **Blackwell Wood**
Kent 2001

In the dim distance a wood on high.

The moon had pierced the hovering cloud and
  lit the Kentish scene.
I rose from my slumber and peered through
  the inn's leaded window.
There, in the dim distance, a wood on high
  so peaceful and serene.
Nightwear was slipped over bare shoulders
  as sleep proved shallow.

Once again it was cosily warm in that ancient wood
  I'd to explore.
A secluded and mysterious hillock where human
  footsteps are rare.
The sun repeated a welcome with dappled delight
  on flora and more.
A breeze teased the leaves on high and one or two
  took to the air.

Fox cubs continued to have fun: one had a tail
  tipped snowy-white.
Glistening trails secreted on seven mossy mounds
  by Roman snails.
Oaks, elms and ash peered to a distant inn that's
  almost out of sight.
Chatty and mischievous squirrels scrambled up
  trees and pulled tails.

The glade remained unchanged; it was eerie
  and unnaturally bare.
Scars on skeletal trunks, bluebells and fungi
  cosseted the ground.
A murky pond and a weeping stream, a sorrowful
  presence there.
Patches of algae clung to a white headstone on
  a hallowed mound.

Golden rays from nature's radiant orb caressed
  neck and shoulders.
Etched epitaphic lines on a tragic stone dimmed
  by toll and time.
'Close to this spot sleeps a hero, his sacrifice
  was witnessed by elders.'
'Pilot Officer Y was one of the Few, so please
  preserve this shrine.'

I set a trio of poppies on his grave and prayed
  his spirit was contented.
Dark clouds gathered with unusual haste and
  the bright sun soon faded.
Light flashed over the memorial and time and
  sleep was transcended.
Did I dream that a Spitfire roared over which
  Pilot Officer Y piloted?

Ibsley
Memories of a Second World War Airfield

A fertile land dotted with farms.

Larks sing on the wing, juicy, grassy-pastures
  with cattle at graze.
Nearby the New Forest, the Avon, a fertile land
  dotted with farms.
Rustics of flora, fauna, and shady groves,
  classical English charms.
Horse and cart, blacksmith, variable weather
  and seasonable days.
In the pre-war Thirties drowsy Ibsley was peaceful,
  always serene.
Life was idyllic with only owls absent from a
  Constable oils scene.

Our Finest Hour, 1940, a German threat to our
  freedom and security.
Daisy and poppy meadows repainted as an airfield
  of three runways.
A row of traditional R.A.F. wooden huts and a
  hanger for repair days.
Enemy's dastardly bombing-runs: metallic birds
  eyed any opportunity.
Hurricanes of 32 Squadron covered convoy patrols
  and then departed.
Spitfires of 118 and 501 Squadrons zoomed-in:
  anxious to get started.

234 Squadron Spitfires complemented and
  contributed to Ibsley Wing.
Famed for 'sweeps' and 'rhubarb-raids' over
  enemy occupied France.
Ground strafing placed enemy radar-operators into
  an anxious trance.
Strategy move from defence to offence and
  delivering a red-hot sting.
Film of 1942 captures David Niven starring in:
  'The First of the Few'.
In addition: 'Bunny' Currant, Brian Kingcombe
  and Tony Bartley too.

Ibsley buried neath a crisp and snowy carpet on
  Christmas Eve 1941.
Panes of frosty diamond-etch at Station
  Headquarters: Moyles Court.
Dickensian scenes on festive cards and merry
  parcels lovingly sought.
Huts of gaiety with dancing and singing as a
  haloed moon looked on.
Sleeping Spitfires tucked under sheeting at rest
  to wait a future flight.
A blessed peace on a crystalline-cold and star-struck
  Christmas night.

Spring awoke with fresh vigour and leaves anew
  upon a truly new Forest.
The clink-clank of spanners together with the
  whirling drills of personnel.
Coughing-spluttering of Merlin engines waiting
  a flighty attacking spell.
Floral fragrances filled the airfield and intoxicated
  senses to their fullest.
A memorable wedding at Ellingham Church one
  fine day in August 1942.
Wing Commander 'Bunny' Currant and Cynthia
  devotedly said: 'I do'.

Scores of service folk with dear memories of
  the house on Cuckoo Hill.
The 1st Fighter Group: 8th U.S.A.A.F. with their
  strange P38 Lightning.
Aero-shape with twin-fuselage and a long
  connecting tail an odd sighting.
R.A.F. Squadrons 66, 118 and 504 arrived with
  Spitfire Vs on their bill.
Aussies and Czechs had squadrons assigned to
  bomber-escort missions.
Combat with F.W.190s and heavy-flak caused
  tragic and stress situations.

The 48th Fighter Group: 9th U.S.A.A.F. covered
  the Normandy invasion.
Thunderbolt fighter-bombers: P47s engaged on
  6th June 1944, 'D'-Day.
In flew 367th Fighter Group of the U.S.A.A.F.
  for an all too short stay.
Ibsley continued to develop and belatedly so in
  an upwardly direction.
The skyward construction of a building for
  observation: a control tower.
Pilots observed war-fields and cities decimated
  by awesome air power.

Repainted as an Instructor's School and a
  Glider-Snatch Training Unit.
Slow winding-down of operations until finality
  in nineteen forty-seven.
Diggers came to excavate sand and gravel and
  scar a once rural heaven.
Was it part of a master plan by Mother Nature
  to help restore and refit?
Glorious with trees and bushes, larks sing and
  lakes sustain fish within.
Name the sailing club: 'Flying Sailor' as tribute
  to star, Andre Jubelin.

In the year of 2000 only the crumbling control
  tower is left standing.
Folk stop on balmy summer evenings to admire
  the picturesque view.
Don't be worried by muffled voices that belong
  to some of the Few.
Merriment of men-of-wings, Forties music,
  it's all so very enchanting.
Nearby the New Forest, the Avon, a fertile land
  dotted with farms.
Rustics of flora, fauna, and shady groves, classical
  English charms.

A tribute to **Wing Commander John Connell Freeborn**
D.F.C.*

John Freeborn.

A gritty straight-talking Yorkshire man from
  Middleton near Leeds.
A streak of Scottish blood that surged during Battle
  of Britain deeds.
Joined the R.A.F. and in October 1938 was posted
  to the Tiger Squadron,
And soon became-as-one with the flight of a
  Spitfire and its Merlin hum.

In action over Dunkirk's beaches as our troops
  made a desperate retreat.
He and his Spitfire destroyed enemy aircraft to
  epitomise our stance to defeat.
A flight of danger and John was hit by a Junkers 88
  and crash-land in France,
To be picked up by a Blenheim and taken to
  England for a second chance.

The Battle of Britain and the planet's fate rested
  in the palms of a few.
Heaven above knew that survival depended on the
  sacrifice of men in blue.
They attacked colossal air-fleets with supreme skill
  and determination,
And we must always remember those flyers from
  our empire and nation.

John fought in the Battle from the start until
  autumn leaves faded and fell.
Scramble upon scramble the Few regularly sounded
  the enemy's death knell.
More sorties and dogfights than anyone who
  defended our dear Mother Isles,
With decorations and merits I proudly read in his
  Battle of Britain files.

Promotion to flight commander with 602 and then
  again to command 118.
So many lost comrades from halcyon days it was
  not fitting to celebrate.
Success rewarded John with the command of the
  illustrious 286 Wing,
And still those aviators sang 'the bells of hell go
  ting-a-ling-a-ling!'

Also in Memory of three of the Few, all 74
Squadron, very good friends of John's who did not
  survive: Pilot Officer Don Cobdon, Pilot Officer
  Peter Chesters and Flying Officer Peter St John.

In memory of **Air Vice Marshal J.E. Johnson** 1915 - 2001
C.B., C.B.E., D.S.O.**, D.F.C.*, Order of Leopold, Croix de Guerre, D.F.C. (USA), U.S. Air Medal, Legion of Merit

Johnnie Johnson.
With thanks to Johnnie for the photograph.

Born at the heart of the country, Barrow-upon-Soar,
  a favourite son of Leicestershire.
His father a policeman, however, it was another
  'highway' Johnnie policed without fear.
A Loughborough Grammar School athlete, strong
  runner and rugged rugby footballer.
Always believed in straight speaking, two of a kind
  and best buddies with Doug Bader.

He came to fame in 1941, and shared glory with
  top-notch fighter pilots of the R.A.F.
They flew sleek and svelte Spitfires, fighter aircraft
  with a punch of power and death!
From Tangmere and her bases in Sussex they
  crossed and tore into a tormented sky.
Strafed occupied territories of northern Europe
  to ensure our cause would never die.

An ace pilot whose victory tally steadily climbed
  and finally peaked at the very top.
A commander leading several squadrons and only
  issued 'two-way tickets' for an 'op'!
He flew with bravery and aplomb, a master
  marksman who inspired all around him.
Diving into the attack or soaring into the heavens,
  a master of flight: a wizard of trim.

A familiar call to arms: 'Tally Ho!' when leaders
  saw enemy aircraft leaving their lair.
The historical call of Leicestershire huntsmen to
  inspire a fighter pilot's do or dare.
Johnnie raved about his flying hours and like the
  best he savoured a good stiff drink.
After 'rhubarbs' it was down to the pub at Bosham
  and soon all were in the pink.

Johnnie was a kindly and forthright man; men of
  his ilk disposed of an evil dictator.
His home county and country will remember him,
  the Barrow-upon-Soar aviator.
It is rumoured that on balmy summer nights at old
  Tangmere laughter can be heard.
Ghosts of young men in the pink and the throb
  of song from a sleek and svelte bird.

A tribute to **Wing Commander K.W. Mackenzie**

D.F.C., A.F.C., A.E.

One of the Few, 1940.

My old friend the bright-eyed Irishman from
  Belfast on the Emerald Isle.
At sixteen years he received a civil 'A' license
  and it can be read on file!
Queen's University to study engineering before
  pitching as a dynamic flyer.
He joined the R.A.F.V.R. and soon W.W.2
  descended with death and fire.

The summer sun of 1940 saw the mother-of-all air
  battles born in the sky.
Churchill's Few against awesome odds with over
  five hundred lads to die.
Our airborne gladiators knew this battle had to be
  won whatever the cost.
Mac's guns with 43 and 501 Squadrons rattled a
  sharp and fiery riposte.

Enemy craft downed as his Hurricane swept over
  West Malling and Kenley.
A Bf109's escape denied by Ken's wingtip prang
  that flipped it into the sea!
On October 25th the Distinguished Flying Cross
  for bravery and other virtues.
Our Ken is one of the finest in any company
  you could wish to choose.

The Battle won and 1941 saw Mac at 247 Squadron
  as a flight commander.
Over Brittany doing a bit of airfield strafing when
  hit and forced to surrender.
His war was over and a German officer packed him
  off to Stalag Luft Three.
At Sagan and as anxious as a bird with clipped
  wings until finally set free.

After the War Ken was promoted to wing commander and chief
instructor on Meteors, serving in the R.A.F. for twenty-eight
meritorious years. An accomplished racing driver he secured
additional fame in 1963 when racing in the Tourist's Trophy race
at the Goodwood track. Finally he held the post of Managing
Director of Air Kenya before retiring to a Mediterranean island.
Ken and his wife now reside in Leicestershire.

In memory of **Flight Lieutenant Roger Hall** 1917 - 2003
D.F.C.

Roger Hall.

Roger and Out

The blazing Hurricane scored a glowing arc across
the noon sky,
And Roger prayed that the emerging pilot would
live and not die.
A seed of sycamore spinning and gyrating on an
autumnal flight,
To England's garden whilst a canopy transformed
fear to delight.

Smokey flying-gear and sizzling cinders on the
sole of a shoe,
Beware of threadbare canopy lines that could
smoulder through.
Surely safety and life are assured as Roger waved
and circled him,
Perhaps a shared evening beer or a wine glass
filled to the brim.

Without warning the descending figure jack-knifed
like a rag doll,
As bullets found flesh and Roger a mere spectator
to the death toll.
Uniform of blue patterned to polka dot with a
buttoned red stain,
A brief encounter wrecked by a Me109 with
pace and no pain.

A silver Spitfire peppered the fighter and the pilot
baled into space,
Falling with debris 'til his parachute opened and
slowed the chase.
Canopy lines of life for an intruder afloat between
death and decent,
Head bowed deserving and expecting Roger's fury
to be spent.

The Hurricane pilot became yet another of
England's seeds set.
His body was found dressed in polka dot clothing
buttoned scarlet.
Just nineteen years of age when he was lowered
to his native earth,
In autumnal sunshine he descended near to the
place of his birth.

(The enemy pilot descended in safety: a life spared.)

In memory of **Group Captain John 'Cats' Eyes' Cunningham** 1917 - 2002
C.B.E., D.S.O.**, D.F.C.*

John Cunningham.

Night Sight

All fair in Thirties' skies, and hedonic flights in a
  Hawker Demon.
An R.A.F. Flying Club, said to be the best plus a
  gin and lemon.
John and Jimmy: 'the little man', ideal companions
  and a great team.
They became two of the Few, after installation of
  a secret beam.
Rumoured to eat many carrots for night-sight
  whilst flying in the dark.
In truth it was Jimmy's little black box and an
  ability to fly as a lark.

Patrolling inky-dark home skies in a stealthy
  Bristol Beaufighter.
Twitchy enemy bomber crews only occasionally
  caught sight of her.
Stars like eyes on a universal face: the magic of
  diamante on black lace.
Engines-max with John in chase: Jimmy 'fixed-on'
  after a word to base.
The PPI on the mysterious cathode ray tube
  uttered a blip, blip, and blip.
Machine-guns fired and a Heinkel's nose began
  to dip, dip, and dip!

1941, and a veritable treble success during the
  night of 15-16th April.
The 7-8th May King George V1th 'tuned-in'
  for a 43 bullet- round kill.
Cats' Eyes stealthily closed to eighty yards before
  delivering a burst.
Cloudscape was no escape for the enemy victim
  of a four gun's thirst.
John's fighter attracted to a searchlight finger,
  as you'd expect a moth.
Mustn't get lost in foul weather associated with
  a low-pressure trough.

'Calling base, calling base: Blazer 24 to Starlight',
  a standard theme.
Chief controller, John 'Brownie' Brown, always
  reassuring and keen.
Mysterious silhouettes, ghostly visions and haloes
  around the moon.
Sagittarius rising, cavernous cloud that seems to
  smother and entomb.
At long last wheels touchdown and a landing as
  sweet as can be.
The two flyers decided that it was time for a
  steaming-hot cup of tea.

Also In memory of **Squadron Leader C.F. 'Jimmy' Rawnsley** 1904 - 1965
D.S.O., D.F.M.*

John a test pilot for De Havilland after victory
 in World War Two.
A superb collection of medals for Cats' Eyes
 and the little man too.
Fully occupied with the Goblin jet engine: great
 work and development.
His skill and experience proved invaluable: a
 perfect complement!
Chief test pilot for the Vampire, Venoms and
 Comets, life was never dull.
Memories of starlit nights, John and Jimmy, and
 a waxing moon at full.

'Bunny' Currant described John Cunningham as one of the finest
men that he ever met. I totally agree with that statement: John
was a real gentleman in the fullest sense.

Jimmy Rawnsley and John Cunningham.
Photographs by kind permission of John Cunningham.

Patrolling inky-dark home skies in a
stealthy Bristol Beaufighter.

In memory of **Wing Commander A.G. Malan** 1910 - 1963
D.S.O.*, D.F.C.*, Croix de Guerre (Belgium and France), Legion d'Honneur, M.C. (Czech)

Flight Lieutenant, 74 Squadron.

Sailor

Born at Wellington in South Africa with a blend
  of Anglo-French blood.
A young man who held self and group discipline
  to be essentially good.
Sailor with a restless spirit employed by the
  Union Castle Steamship Line,
He adjusted bearings to encompass values of
  decency and candour so fine.

Why exchange his love of briny ocean waves
  for lofty airwaves on high?
In 1935 he entered the R.A.F. and roared with
  the 'Tigers' into the sky.
So apt for a leader and top-gun to blend into
  74 Squadron when war came,
Presenting opportunities to hunt the enemy and
  keep them on a tight rein.

Dunkirk dogfights and Spitfire sweeps in his
  machine-gun decked rapier.
Off duty softly spoken and given to pampering
  his black and white terrier.
The Battle of Britain's Few were glorious in
  the powdery blue skies above,
Where the dynamics of aerial warfare claimed
  many a life and lost love.
Sailor tops with tactics and his claims were high
  and squadron losses few.
The enemy were savaged during that endless
  summer and Dowding knew.
Malan was a man's man and a trusted leader and
  his pilots respected him,
But Dorniers and Heinkels tried to blast our
  cities when skies grew dim.

In the dark of June 19th 1940 searchlights trained
  glaring fingers on raiders.
Over southern suburbs the droning aircraft were
  feared malicious invaders.
Sailor took to the inky-black runway and searched
  in the burning city glow,
And upon locating the Heinkel 111s let reddish
  bullets finish off the show.

In March '41 the ace pilot took command of the
  esteemed Biggin Hill Wing.
He led forays over Europe and increased his tally
  by draining the Nazi sting!
One of our best and bravest fighter pilots when
  our country was in dire needs,
So sad he left during days of peace but joy in
  the memory of his daring deeds.

(Sailor was born on the 3rd October 1910 and died of
Parkinson's disease on 17th September 1963 at the terribly
early age of 52.)

Saucy Antics At Croydon, 1940

From the memoirs of Wing Commander C.F. 'Bunny' Currant D.S.O., D.F.C.*, Croix de Guerre

Croydon Airfield 1940.

Bunny hungered for our country's success during
the Battle of Britain.
Hurricane and Spitfire aeroplanes fed pride and
security to every citizen.
Soldiers will march better and fighter pilots sleep
better on full stomachs.
It was an unwritten fact: fish and chips invariably
left Jerry flummoxed!

Nazi scientists delved deeply to locate the magical
top-secret ingredient.
They concluded it was a spicy brown sauce labelled
'H.P.' by expedient.

During the 1940 Battle, our Bunny sat at readiness
awaiting his meal.
A sprinkle of salt, a shower of vinegar and a shake
of H.P. to set the seal.
Catastrophe as the bottle-top was loose and brown
fluid took to the air.
Amid a thousand curses a ceiling dripped and a
light carpet took a share.

Scramble! An angry and hungry Bunny zoomed
off to clobber the Hun.
Grisly mood was warranted as Jerry again
interrupted his fish and chip fun.

There is an important lesson to be understood
when involved in any war.
Never disturb your adversaries during mealtime
or you'll suffer for sure.

*(Perhaps Bunny shot down an enemy flyer to
satisfy his anger and hunger)*

*(Bunny says that the Luftwaffe invariably
came over at mealtime)*

Royal Airforce **Tangmere**
West Sussex

Jim Hallows, one of Tangmere's flying stars. He know rests in Tangmere churchyard.
With thanks to Ken Mackenzie for the photograph.

The grace of early twentieth century Tangmere set
  in Sussex's finest glades.
A wise old windmill sat on the hill over-looking
  farmland and grassy blades.
1917's creation of an airfield to raid the Western
  Front with bullet and bomb.
The next year an R.A.F. base and several squadrons
  trained with aplomb.

If perchance one balmy late summer's evening
  you visit... do stop and listen.
Don't be concerned if you see ghosts or hear the
  firing of an engine piston.
Avro 504s, Sopwith Pups and Dolphins dive and
  climb with engine coughs.
You may see Gloster Gamecocks skirting a waxing
  moon like giant moths,
Or flying pageants in strict wing formation and
  linked by cotton streamers.
They may be piloted by the lingering souls of 43
  Squadron's past dreamers.
Many an enthusiast yearns for the halcyon days of
  the Twenties and Thirties.
Year '39 heard Holst's 'Mars': the bringer of war
  to host the violent Forties.

Action stations: scramble and Hurricanes strove
 desperately to gain height.
Maxim: 'Near enough was never good enough'
 when involved in a dogfight.
Across the Channel came waves of hostile Dorniers,
 Me109s and Heinkels.
Aces such as Frank Carey, Caesar Hull and Jim
 Hallows chalked up vital kills.
Few recall the devastation of a Stuka-bomber
 attack on the 16th August 1940.
The metal birds with a swastika emblem battered
 Tangmere whilst on a sortie.
Fierce explosions and tongues of reddish flame
 veiled by a choking smoke.
Damaged buildings and aircraft can always be
 repaired but not so dead folk!
During that vital Battle of Britain R.A.F. Tangmere
 was always hard pressed.
Vital success was thanks to the Few: pilots who
 helped many to pass the test.

The painful chats about friends who 'bought it'
 to solid earth or briny blue.
The pinnacle of pleasures when renewing old
 friendships and starting anew.
1944 with Tangmere squadrons covering Dieppe
 and the beaches on D-Day.
V1 rockets meant daring and timely interceptions
 to keep doodlebugs at bay.
The frontline airfield served our country to the
 highest standards possible.
Motto: 'Attack to Defend' and her efforts ensured
 that victory was inevitable.

Post-war Tangmere revealed the power and
 potential of the age of the Jet.
World War 2 battle experienced pilots with world
 air speed records to be set.
Teddy Donaldson blazed a trail across the sky
 in his fighter: the Meteor.
The ace pilot, Neville Duke smashed a rapid reply
 with his Hawker Hunter.

The summer of 1999 and runways, hangers and huts
 have all but gone.
A lonely control tower is crumbling, it's missing
 the bright lights that shone.
Where are the renowned main-gates and classic
 buildings that stood there?
A housing estate and ploughed fields is all that
 remains of R.A.F. Tangmere.

If perchance one balmy late summer's evening you
 visit... do stop and listen.
Don't be concerned if you see ghostly, youthful
 eyes that twinkle and glisten.
Neckerchiefs, thick fleecy leather jackets and the
 faint aroma of pipe smoke.
The laughter of Dispersal hut humour and Johnnie's
 always first with a joke.

What joy as I find a brilliant museum with
 photographs and memories of old!
Once again the nostalgia of Spitfires, Hurricanes
 and Sopwith Pups in the fold.
As the years pass by and age transports our heroes
 up to stars that never fade,
Rest assured that early morning breezes will
 always caress this Sussex glade.

In memory of **Squadron Leader Michael E.A. Royce** 1919 - 1998

Michael in 1940.

Scruffy

Michael could never be described as a prima donna.
For him such superficialities really didn't matter.
Never the neatest and certainly not the smartest
   of men.
Not attired as Cary Grant but girls still saw him
   as a gem.

A newspaper made merry of his appearance in
   pilot days.
Was sharp and smart enough during the 1940
   Battle phase.
Jerry took him seriously when engaged in
   aerial fights.
One of the Few and who could achieve
   greater heights?

Always a screwdriver in his pockets 'till
   holes appeared.
Who knows when mechanical items need to
   be repaired?
Loosen one screw and tighten one in case
   it's forgotten.
Never adjusted his tie or noticed he was missing
   a button.

He laughed at his caricature sketched by friends
   now gone.
Whatever his task he was a perfectionist and
   this shone.
A man of fine qualities and not an ounce of
   vainglory inside.
Both man and cartoon adored by those close
   to his side.

Michael attaching parachute, 1940.

Summer Of Dappled Shade

The summer sun of 1940 blazed with a warm
　and golden glow,
　So vanquishing the memory of a cruel winter
　and suffocate snow.
A band of young men of gladiatorial spirit served
　us dear at war,
Fighting for our country whilst outnumbered two
　to the score.

Remember the pilots who flew their
　streamlined aeroplanes,
And the service teams with the men who
　extinguished flames.
Grassy-meadows or farmer-sowed strips always
　a relieving sight,
For men with shattered dials or engines spluttering
　from a fight.

Our flyers stood fast and firm against swastika-
　marked marauders,
And smashed and crashed German Messerschmitts
　and Dorniers.
Yet another scrambled take-off to soar into colossal
　blue skyways,
As dogfights bloodied and tainted the white cirrus
　of the highways.

During intervals of peace a few of the Few lounged
　in deckchairs,
Read books or wrote confidential letters home to
　allay family fears.
Hundreds of their number died never having flown
　a victory parade,
But rest neath mature trees born during a summer
　of dappled shade.

A quick re-fit. Thanks to Tom Neil for the photograph.

In memory of **Flight Lieutenant Raymond Holmes**

SERGEANT RAY HOLMES

Thanks to Geoff Nutkins for the photograph.

Sky Spy

The Liverpool Exchange, Liver Birds and dear
old Skerry's.
A newspaper reporter, fresh and breezy as the
Mersey ferries.
Off to a Scotland airbase with V.R. tie and uniform
to learn to fly.
No webs over Prestwick as a Tiger Moth fluttered
in the sky.

A fighter pilot in 1940 with 504 Squadron and
silver wings.
Their song: 'Room five-hundred and four':
as Vera Lynn sings.
Ray a member of the Band of Brothers known
as the Few.
His 'Buckingham Palace Dornier' despatched
from an angry blue.
Headlines: "Tell dad I'm O.K." after a shaky
'caterpillar' flight.
Geoff Nutkins captures it on canvas: a historic
and splendid sight.

Ray recalls flying by instruments on the darkest
of nights.
A stressful time indeed when coned by your
own searchlights.
Wily plan to capture an enemy aircraft plus a
French connection.
Fortunately for our Ray the scheme met its death
at conception.
Memories of friends with Squadron Leader John
Sample to the fore.
Never to forget close pals, Sid Ireland, Jaggers
or jolly Wag Haw.

A perilous convoy destined for Archangel via
a meander to Iceland.
Pontoon and poker with chums Icke and Vyle
serving a good hand.
Five months endurance with short days and
crystalline Russian snow.
Hurricanes over Murmansk in support of allies
against a common foe.
The novelty of locals with silver teeth, forget
vodka at R.A.F. Kremlin.
A frozen wilderness of a land, requiring
navigation by dead reckonin'.

A return home to a base near Oxford and flying
  Spitfires as a sky-rider.
Rising to tip-top heights and then lean lows for
  our daring Deesider.
Decidedly dangerous camera shots often scooped:
  they never told a lie.
Flight Lieutenant Raymond Holmes forever famed
  as the SKY SPY.

Skerry's College, Rodney Street, Liverpool.
He was an old boy of the School.
Sky Spy: name of his book.

Squadron 'flying duty' blackboard. Image kindly supplied by Sylvia Royce.

Michael Royce playing his
gramaphone. Photograph kindly
supplied by Sylvia Royce.

Squadron Scramble

Dedicated to The FEW: the aircrew who flew in The Battle of Britain of 1940

Jimmy is new to the squadron, athletic, nineteen
   and with ginger hair.
He is calmly confident, likeable, not long trained:
   so short in prayer.
We sit in a Kentish field by Dispersal: close to
   a runway of cut grass.
Once more and by noon we'll doubtless meet
   the Luftwaffe en-masse.

The blinding sun often warns us of the Devil's
   final sting.
Do the bells of hell really go ting - a - ling - a ling?

Scramble! Squadron Scramble! Scramble!
Who's to live and who's to die in life's
   flighty gamble?
I ditch my briar-pipe and sprint towards
   the aeroplane.
My fitter secures the chute and helps to strap
   me in again.
I flick on the ignition switch: a good
   positive contact.
A Merlin cough - swirl of smoke -
   an agreeable pact.
I'm entombed as jittery hands close my
   cockpit hood.
Plug in for transmission: receive message
   and understood.

Gun sight on, oxygen on, all instruments addressed.
Brain totally focussed for the forthcoming acid test.
Chocks away.
Soon I'll be in the fray!

I turn into the wind and push the throttle forward.
Faster and faster until willing wings take
 me skyward.
Wind wheels up and pull back the stick,
 desperate for height.
Always tried to attack out of the sun, give the
 bandits a fright!
Controller announces: '100 plus bombers at
 15,000 feet'.
'Steer 195 degrees Angels 15' then Tally-ho
 to meet.

I spot a large enemy formation about
5000 feet below.
My heart is pounding in anticipation and I yell:
 'Tally-Ho!'.
I kick the rudder: bank sharply and give the
 stick a push.
Gathering speed rapidly and dive for a real
 adrenaline rush.
Gun button to fire: oh the thrill of leading an attack.
A three-second burst puts a Junkers 88 on the rack!

All around are trails of smoke and flashes of flame.
Bullets, bombs, and cannons with lives to claim.
Jimmy has a 90-degree attack and a two
 second burst.
Like a hot wire through cheese he bags his first!
A 109 is diving vertically in a fit of death throes.
To all intents a wounded wasp with a yellow nose.
Jimmy, Jimmy, look out, behind you, I just yelled!
Oh, he's bought it, going down like a tree
 just felled.
Out of ammunition, low on fuel so I'll return
 to base.
A set of parents to be informed of a missing face.

The blinding sun often warns us of the Devil's
 final sting.
Do the bells of hell really go ting - a - ling - a ling?

Tom is new to the squadron, tall, nineteen and
 with black hair.
He is calmly confident, likeable, not long trained:
 so short in prayer.
We sit in a Kentish field by Dispersal: close to
 a runway of cut grass.
Once more and by noon we'll doubtless meet
 the Luftwaffe en-masse.

Co-Written by: Wing Commander C.F. 'Bunny' Currant
and Michael Kendrick.

(Inspired by a great friend)

Dedicated to **Squadron Leader B.G. 'Stapme' Stapleton**
D.F.C. and Dutch D.F.C.

Squadron Leader Gerald Stapleton

Gerald Stapleton

An entrant to 603 Edinburgh Squadron with
　its axiom: 'If you dare.'
A brightly sharp South African eminently suitable
　for the hemisphere.
"Stapme, what a filly" gorgeous Jane the
　newspaper cartoon starlet,
So eagerly read by many a red-blooded Battle of
　Britain fighter pilot.

Enemy action over Scotland, and then a squadron
　shift to Hornchurch.
Stapme calm and solid, always there to support a
　colleague in the lurch.
To reminisce: Uncle George, Rusty, Richard Hillary
　and Brian Carbury,
'Bubbles', 'Popper' Pease, 'Sheep' and especially
　good old 'Ras' Berry.

Stapme's crash-landing in a hop-field so adroit
　and deliberately directed.
Naturally a family at picnic with a refreshing
　cuppa - gratefully accepted.

25,000 feet and innocently in echelon with twenty
　Messerschmitt 109s.
Rapidly spiralled-down and gladly tracked the
　Torquay to Paddington line.

Franz von Werra could not escape the resolute
　guns of the South African.
'The One that got Away' will never apply to a
　fighter-flyer called Stapleton.

Stapme accompanied Brian Carbury and also
　Richard Hillary in his flight.
'The Last Enemy': Richard's true and fateful
　account of youthful plight.

The Distinguished Flying Cross awarded to our
　hero: worthy recipient.
A pilot of the Few who fought with dogged daring:
　bravery inherent.
Many decades passed when news emerged of
　Rusty's final resting place.
Nationwide memories of a sister and the survival
　of a Forties watch face.

Stapme's four crossings over a tempestuous Atlantic
　without even a blip.
Served with the M.S.F.U. and every time gave the
　enemy 'U'-Boats the slip.
257 Squadron posting and keenly tasted action in
　the formidable Typhoon.
As commander of 247 Squadron he filled the Huns
　with a mood of doom.

December '44 and he dived for a rocket attack on
an enemy troop-train.
A whirl of fire and the loco' exploded and fatally
damaged his aeroplane.
It coughed, shuddered, and then lost height to a
fatally punctured radiator.
Captured, questioned, then prison-life at Stalag
Luft 1 for our avid aviator.

Post-war career as a B.O.A.C. pilot and often
skirted West African routes.
Time to reflect and recall pals who wore blue
uniforms and flying boots.
An entrant to 603 Edinburgh Squadron with its
axiom: 'If you dare.'
A brightly sharp South African eminently suitable
for the hemisphere.

Stapme was an ace pilot during the 1940 Battle of Britain indeed
he was one of the frontline Few. The skill, sacrifice and bravery
of those young pilots has been recorded for future posterity,
indeed their names are now legendary and are written in the
annals of history.

In the summer of 2002 the author David Ross, famous for
his superb book – 'Richard Hillary – the definitive biography',
launched a second, brilliant biography of which it is not
necessary for me to quote the obvious title.

"From this day to the ending of the world,
But we in it shall be remembered;
We few, we happy few, we band of brothers."
(Henry 5th)

(Stapme, thank you for your many kind words in
respect of my poetry)

Stapme and grandson.

Steady Hands

One day during the 1940 Battle of Britain

Raiders over London, 1940.

The hands were level at twenty-to-eight on the
old church clock.
A farmer was sitting on a five bar gate checking
out his sleepy flock.
The summer sun was rising gently over ancient
Wealden meadows.
Fleeting images across ripening crops were simply
cloud shadows.

A distant drone was heard from shores beyond
those Kentish Downs.
Silhouettes in echelon formation were targeting
old English towns.
Deadly roar at eighteen thousand feet from lots
of twin-engine craft.
There were many more but they possessed a
single propeller shaft.

An armada of Dorniers with guns supplying
maximum covering fire.
Loaded with explosives to convert a town or city
into a funeral pyre.
Our early warning radar was a great help and the
Observer Corps too.
Once again our saviour would be Fighter
Command: Churchill's Few.

The waspish Messerschmitt 109 fighter in speedy
schwarms would fly.
Sometimes they would chalk contrails across the
smoky and hazy sky.
An umbrella escort of quality pilots like Moelders
or Wick and Galland.
Achtung Spitfeur they would exclaim over our
green and pleasant land.

Tally-Ho came the call as Royal Air Force fighters
dived into the attack.
Like hawks they stalked the bombers and selected
targets from the pack.
Gun button to fire then a burst when in range and
gauged in a gun-sight.
The Dornier shuddered and then belched an oily
smoke and lost height.

The flame-filled cockpit of a Hurricane leader as
it spiralled to earth.
Joy on the face of a wingman when he saw a
parachute touch the turf.
Smoke trails are the Devil's cobwebs as they
create scars on white cloud.
A Junkers 88 in a death dive and the Channel
offered a foamy shroud.

Fierce aerial battles sent reverberations across
  an angry blue heaven.
Six bandits came-in from-out of the sun attacking
  high at about eleven.
Battles raged through misty mountains and valleys
  of cavernous cloud.
The chatter of machine-gun bursts and violent
  explosions incredibly loud.

'Widge' Gleed returned to base out of ammo
  and drenched in perspiration.
Extra bacon and eggs to recharge his batteries
  for the next confrontation.
Re-armed and re-fuelled by a dedicated service
  team on the ground.
A scrambled take-off and a soaring climb to
  make Gleed's heart pound.

A solitary Spitfire was hit with the inexperienced
  pilot trying to climb.
The victim of a twin-engine fighter that had a
  forward cannon sublime.
Shells peppered the rookie pilot across his wing
  and punctured the nose.
Glycol splattered a veil across the cockpit as
  a prelude to death throws.

The immortal Tuck led a head-on attack against
  a formidable formation.
The bravest of the brave and every day further
  enhanced his reputation.
His Browning's pumped hot lead and a Heinkel
  dramatically imploded.
An adjacent friend in formation wing tipped and
  two bombers exploded!

Magnificent young men ensured our future and
  our freedom - the Few.
The much vaunted and proud Luftwaffe was
  beaten and well they knew.
What greater glory can be offered to our illustrious
  Fighter Command?
Don't forget pilots like Dennis David, Tuck,
  'Ginger', 'Stapme' and band.

The summer weeks passed and autumn months
  were gradually fading.
A farmer was sitting on a five bar gate content
  after market trading.
'Bunny' Currant a respected fighter ace checked
  his watch after a sortie.
The hands were level at twenty-to-eight or a
  military nineteen-forty: 1940.

'Widge' Gleed.

The Autumn Leaves

A reflection on the events of the Battle of Britain

The 1940 Battle of Britain saw daggers drawn
  on the world's highest stage.
Yes our fighter pilots were the empire's brightest
  and cleverest of their age.
Youthful confidence and vitality had been in
  abundance when spring was new.
There was victory pride for the survivors but
  losses spawned heartaches too.

Air raids over London and southern counties saw
  death dressed as an inferno.
Kent's meadows scarred and cratered by war:
  fire consumed debris on show.
What irony that the summer sun painted home
  skies and seas so very blue.
Azure above and below completed an orbital
  horizon for the legendary Few.

The Battle was won when autumn's harvest was
  due to receive thanks giving.
Not all our young and weary pilots blossomed or
  matured under skies shining.
Sparkling morning dews had raised and refreshed
  well-worn grassy runways,
Where past flyers had left dead-men's footprints
  and chocks scarred other bays.

Over five hundred of their number departed our
  airways and all heaven bound.
We had forever lost their exuberance and that
  was irreparable and profound.
Maybe Charles Darwin was right about evolution
  and the survival of the fittest,
But he failed to make allowances for God's
  bravest and sacrifice of the finest.

A dreaded telegram and a knock on the door:
  loss of a sergeant or pilot officer.
Next day the squadron leader bought it, his
  medals never left his wife's dresser.
The eternal love-light there to see in her eyes
  on annual visits to the village.
For sixty years she took flowers to her husband's
  grave on pilgrimage.

The early autumn frosts of that fateful year tinged
  the leaves with some regret.
Those summer leaves had witnessed the daily
  dogfights and seen the blood-let.
Would human memory lack gratitude for pilots
  and witnesses sixty years on?
Nature's beauty of forest reds, rusts and gold
  commemorate seasonal rotation.

September 15th 2000 and black, ginger or whatever
  colour of hair is now grey.
Manly frames are not so strong and some of the
  muscles have 'slimmed' away.
But follow the sharply observant eyes and chat
  about their reminiscences too.
They are some of the empire's best and collectively
  they are called the Few.

May my prose be dedicated to all the brotherhood
  above and may it be eternal.
Whatever future battles come to pass they will
  never again be so vital or pivotal.
Mnemonically the rainbow reminds us of God's
  declaration and promise to us all,
So please remember the Few when autumn leaves
  turn to gold and start to fall.

Memories of a Fighter Pilot

The poems of Wing Commander C.F. 'Bunny' Currant

Wick, Scotland April 1940

One warm spring Scottish day
when bees were flexing wings,
disturbed by throb of engines' roar
whoosh of propellers spinning;
two fighters taxied, turned and stopped
both pointing into the wind.

The pilots sat in cockpits strapped,
be-helmeted and goggled,
feet on rudders, hand on stick,
they looked liked twins together:
thumbs-up given, throttles wide
the planes first slowly stirred.

Then rushing on in gathering speed
their shapes were swiftly blurred.
Up, up we climbed above the fields
criss-crossed with hedge and wall
as sheep and cattle grazed in peace
not disturbed by us at all.

The sky was blue with tufts
of cotton-wool-like cloud,
we banked and climbed and turned
in majesty so proud.
Each pilot's trust held firm and true
two friends of bonded spirit.

*The artist, one of Bunnys'
own paintings.*

Not knowing then that one would die
in short, swift-shattered minute
as suddenly as jarring jolt,
a rending, tearing crack
and plummeting towards the earth
an aircraft on its back.

A wing flew off, a crazy spin;
it plunged through air so still
and jagged metal tore the earth
beside a Scottish hill:
And so he died. Whilst I lived on
to land and be released.

With axes rushed from ambulance
they cut my cockpit creased,
with hurried word I told them
of the aerial collision,
the unseen plane that slid across
my cockpit's Perspex sheen.

They buried him in a Scottish grave,
a group of pilots there,
his coffin lowered into the earth
cap and badge upon the bier,
as evening light waned in the west
a cornet shrilled its call
to close the scene of one young life,
be-flagged with bearer's pall.

France- May 1940

From Scottish air to foreign skies
to search o'er Northern France.
The squadron flew to quarters new,
to Hawkinge where, perchance,
we'd take off in the spring-like dawn
to help to stem the tide
of Panzer troops and Nazi hordes
that swept their foes aside.

Billowing oily, blackened smoke
showed where the battle lay
as engines sprang to life to lift
each pilot on his way:
to look, to seek, to twist and turn
in skies of azure blue
high over mass of German grey
and scattered French poilu.

German bombers appeared in view
about to spill their hate,
I saw the bombs float through the air
to burst in ordered gait
across the woods and in the roads
to spout in deadly plume
and splash hot jagged bits of steel
that sent men to their doom.

Fierce anger gripped me like a vice
to spur me on to fight,
I flew in close behind these three
and got one in my sight,
as bullets ripped from barrels' spouts
the Heinkel smoked and fell
but not before the enemy guns
had sounded engine's knell.

The motor seized, propeller stopped
and fumes curled round my face,
they filled the cockpit in a fog
and bitter was the taste:
a sharp loud bang and harness off
I clambered to bale out;
a change of mind, I slipped back in,
to steer towards the ground.

To crash-land on the soil of France
and smash my face about-
a broken nose, a loosened tooth,
a gash across my cheek,
as farming folk with helping hand
washed wounds at nearby creek
then set me on my northward route
away from closing Hun,
to catch a boat from Calais, home-
another day's work done.

Bunny's own painting of him chasing a Junkers 88 in 1940.

Bunny left at the wedding of Paul Edge. Archie McKellar stands next to the bride.

Croydon- September 1940

Then yet again I took the air,
when Croydon was my base
to fight it out in fear and sweat
so many times each day:
to smell the burn of cordite flash,
to see the flames of war
high up above the fields of Kent
the dive, the zoom, the soar.

Returning from a clash with foes
one day I came across
a sight that burnt deep in my soul
and never can be lost.
A pilot dangling from his 'chute
towards the earth did drift
I circled round this friend or foe
so helplessly alone:

A watch to keep if any dared
to fire on such a gift,
it was a useless gesture though
as round and round I flew
I saw as in an awful dream
first smoke, and then flames spew,
curl up his back as arms he waved
and burn the cords of life
to snap the body from the 'chute
and snatch him from war's strife.

With sickening horror in my heart
I landed back at base
and cried myself to sleep that night,
in thanks to God's good grace
that I was spared yet once again,
to live and fight this fight
against the things I saw as wrong,
for things I knew were right.

Westhampnett November 1941

The days wore on, another year,
by this time squadron leader
of Spitfire squadron five-o-one
with pilots young and eager,
to shepherd bombers on their way
to strike at German dump.
This was our task as once more asked
a flock of fighters flew
just on the wave tops dirty grey
the battle to renew.

Pull on the stick and lift her up
to clear the chalk cliffs barrier,
and down again to hug the ground
like predatory harrier.
Before the target was achieved
a wall of fog closed tight
to clamp me like a spider's web
cocooned and blind with fright.

I found myself in steep left bank,
my eyes could not discern
the instruments of climb and dive,
of level, bank and turn.
They made no sense to brain: so tense
that imminence of death
made all my actions seem quite sane,
as with a bated breath:

I took my feet off redder bar,
my hand off stick as well
and folded arms across my chest
and waited for the knell.
The end was magic ne'er forgot
as suddenly I found
myself in sunshine clear and safe
a few feet off the ground.
I climbed away and headed home
my sweating flesh to dry
and landed back on English soil:
another day gone by.

From left to right: Frank Carey, 'Bunny' Currant, 'Grumpy' Unwin, Dennis David, 'Cats Eyes' Cunningham and Bob Doe. Biggin Hill, 1990.

Memories of a Fighter Pilot

The poems of Wing Commander C.F. 'Bunny' Currant Continued

Redhill-March 1942

Until in nineteen forty-two,
high over Northern France
we hoped to lure the Germans up
to try our skill and chance.
We used some bombers as bait
to bring them closely in-
the trap worked well and on they came
black crosses set on wing.

And in the fight that filled the sky
I found myself alone with three
Focke Wulfs upon my tail,
their guns ablaze with lead
as bullets smashed my instruments
and one went in my head,
I felt the warmth of blood and sweat
run down my hair and neck.

So down I dived in swifter plunge
to get close to the deck
as down and down I hurtled on,
I looked back on my tail
to see the flash of German guns
pour out their deadly hail.
The earth rushed up to put a stop
to screaming howling dive:

I bent in two and pulled her through
to zoom-up and survive.

I weaved and jerked in desperate thought
and prayed to God aloud,
I didn't want to die like this,
I didn't want to go:
and looking back I saw the grim
black crosses of the foe.

They let me be to get back free
to cross the Channel grey
with fearful heart and sickly pain
I headed west for home.
I turned the tap on: oxygen pack
to breathe and hope to pray
this engine sound would keep me bound
for distant friendly coast.

For pure white cliffs that always seemed
like splendid welcome host,
for waves of green that nature's scene
would turn to fields of hay,
for native soil which gave such joy
in which to live and play
it seemed an age ere pilot caged
in Spitfire's lovely shape
saw chequered earth of his birth
in patterns down below,
revealing there the larger square
where airfield shape did show.

Throttling back with lowered flaps
I circled in a glide,
locking tight the shoulder straps
that held me safe inside.
Fingers flipped selector switch
and wheels dropped into place
as airfield hedge slid underneath
and grass rose up in grace
to meet the final flattening out, of
aircraft's slowing pace.

But bullet-punctured rubber tyres
caused wheels to bite in deep
and in a flash there came the crash
of somersaulted heap:
and all was silent save the hiss
of liquid on hot metal,
something which to weary nerves
meant only deadly petrol
spilling from the smothered wreck
of Spitfire upside down:

Holding taut so was I caught
and struggled like a clown,
terrified that strapped inside
I'd be a flame-hungry meal
before the crews who rushed to help
could lift the wreckage clear,

but powerful arms with heave and strain
gave me room to move,
I crawled away and felt strong hands
my elbows firmly steer.

To guide me to a stretcher close,
to speed me on my way
to hospital in Folkestone there
to wait and think. I lay
with thoughts that death was near at hand,
to ponder on my wound,
would I survive or would I die?
I prayed and I felt much moved.

As white-clad figures wheeled me in
to operate and probe
on tabletop, so still I lay.
Needle pierced my flesh,
and anaesthetic washed my mind
from all its fears so fresh,
from all the vivid coloured strains
that bit into my soul,
from all the longings in my heart
for life and victory whole.

All of the above poems were composed in 1945
by Wing Commander C.F. 'Bunny' Currant D.S.O. D.F.C.*
Croix de Guerre.

Wing Commander Christopher Frederick Currant
14th December 1911 12th March 2006.

'Bunny' was born at Luton and educated at Rydal Public School. One of several siblings, he lost an elder sister whilst climbing the Matterhorn in the Swiss Alps.

Joining the R.A.F. in 1936 he became great pals with Jock Muirhead. They delighted in flying Gloster Gauntlets: "Exploring God's cavernous and mountainous clouds, one of the happiest times of my life." Later in Hurricanes the pair were posted to 605 Squadron and provided cover for the Dunkirk evacuation. Over Arras on May 22nd his Hurricane was hit by return fire, resulting in a crash landing.

When Luftflotte 5 attacked northeast England 605 Squadron created havoc among enemy bombers over Newcastle; Bunny shot down two (possibly three) Heinkel 111s, with Leader Archie McKellar equalling that score: "One of the bravest and finest pilots I ever flew with, a wee marvel of a man!"

During a hectic September at Croydon, Bunny destroyed a minimum of twelve enemy aircraft over southeast London and Kent. 'Jock' Muirhead D.F.C. went down with his aircraft on October 15th with Bunny describing him as: "A Lion with Wings!" Starting a second tour in August 1941: commanding 501 Squadron, he appeared in the classic film: 'First of the Few', as himself. He told me: "The only time that I lost my life."

Bunny led his Spitfires on 'Rhubarbs' and escorted allied bombers on many raids. He was shot-up by three Focke-Wulf Fw 190s: cannon shells smashed most of his instruments, with one shell lodging in his skull. He skimmed the Channel waves and crash landed at Lympne on the Kent coast: "My tyres were punctured, I somersaulted over and blood oozed down my face, and then I heard the hiss of petroleum on hot metal. I thought I was a 'gonna', until I heard the bell on the fire-engine, then prayed!"

Recovering in a west-county hospital he enjoyed the company of Richard Hillary (author of: 'The Last Enemy'). "He had a brilliant mind, but his hands were dreadfully burnt and should never have been allowed to fly again."

On July 7th was awarded the D.S.O. (A most courageous and brilliant leader.) He was also awarded the Belgium Croix de Guerre in April 1943, and was twice mentioned-in-despatches. Bunny's Wing covered the 'D'-Day beaches on 6th June 1944 and onto Normandy.

In 1954 he was assigned to the Royal Norwegian Air Force Staff College and stayed for four years. Held in high regard he was officially knighted: 'Order of St. Olaf '.

Bunny umpired many times in the 1950/60s for Wimbledon fortnight; full of praise for the skill and sportsmanship of the Rod Laver and Newcomb's of this world.

A very fine golfer, playing well into his late eighties he was, indeed, a talented painter and a lover of literature. Bunny was so looking forward to the launch of this book! Sadly missed!

Dedicated to Sergeant Pilot H. 'Bert' Black 32, 257 and 46 Squadrons

A pilot from Ibstock in Leicestershire

Bert Black in 1940.

The Fallen Few Of 1940

We must never forget the fallen Few:
  the lost five hundred.
They sacrificed their young lives for you, you.

Clad in leather jackets, boots, scarves, helmets
  and goggles.
All afraid but they conquered their fear, fear.

A fated summer sky aflame with debris and
  smoke trails.
A sad arena with many touches of blue, blue.

Under green turf they lie or in the depths of
  a Channel bed.
The memory of the fallen Few so dear, dear.

It was Gwen Black, the widow of Bert, who wrote the Forward for the brilliant book: 'The Battle of Britain Then and Now,' edited by Winston G. Ramsey.

We were good friends for many years until she recently passed away. The above photograph was always positioned opposite to where her favourite chair was. Gwen and Bert were childhood friends and she never remarried.

Herbert Black was born on the 12th June 1914 at Measham. He grew up at Ibstock and attended the village's Junior School, winning a scholarship to The Dixie Grammar School at Market Bosworth. The school was founded in 1320 and one famous master was the writer Dr. Samuel Johnson.

Played for the School's Cricket Team (possibly others), and also for Leicestershire Mixed County Hockey Team.
Pre-war: a weights and measures inspector at Coalville and a pilot with the R.A.F.V.R.

Served with 226 Squadron in the 1940 'Battle of France' and flew Hurricanes with 32 and 257 Squadrons in the 'Battle of Britain.' He was shot down on the 29th October 1940, and died at Ashford Hospital on the 9th November 1940. His wife, Gwen, was by his side, ignoring an air raid that raged overhead.

The Few

Blue One in 1940.

On patrol at twenty thousand feet the six Spitfires
  spotted one hundred plus.
Radio Transmission had alerted Blue One and they
  homed in with little fuss.
They attacked-line abreast - withholding fire
  until two hundred yards.
As always the ace was high however this was no
  game of cards!
Blue One was in control and totally focussed as
  were the other five.
Bullets ripped into enemy craft and several turned
  into a steep death dive.
Return-fire from the enemy fleet caught Red Two
  in the fuel tank.
God blessed him as he erupted into a sheet of flame
  as he tried to bank.
Six enemy bombers crashed to swampy deaths
  around Romney Marsh.
The five Spitfires knew the opposing fighters'
  punishment would be harsh.
Eighty plus Me 109s came in from a glaring
  canopy on high.
Shells and bullets hailed from a hazy sun and four
  Spitfires had to die.
All alone was Blue One, beads of perspiration
  trickled from under his helmet.
Frantically he turned to the left and then the right
  but his outcome was set.

A Heinkel drifted into his line-of-fire and a two
  second burst killed the metal bird.
It smoked, flamed, then lost height, and exploded
  with a force quite absurd.
Suddenly Blue One's instruments shattered and
  yellow flame licked all about.
His speedy friend responded one last time as it fell
  on its back and spilled him out.
Down he plummeted with the enemy still around
  until he pulled his ripcord.
With a flap and a jerk the parachute opened: but he
  could yet be put to the sword!
He descended to five thousand feet when an enemy
  fighter suddenly dived.
Blue One saw wingtips flicker light and then
  darkness: he never survived.
How the Few emblazoned the summer skies of
  1940 with skill and self-sacrifice.
Lady Luck was often needed when death was
  sanctioned by the toss of a dice.

A dedication to **Wing Commander R.F.T. Doe**
D.S.O., D.F.C.*

Bob Doe.
With thanks to Bob for the photograph.

"Michael,
I wouldn't have missed the Battle of Britain for the world!"
(Quote from Bob)

The Fighter Pilot

Our mid-twentieth century knights had
  elliptical wings and flew high,
Shepherding over a human flock for which
  they were prepared to die.
Azure English sky, dazzling sunlight and
  colonies of cloud castles.
A pulsating orbital arena, rapid heartbeats
  in vital 1940 aerial battles.

Firm footprints visible on sparkling grass-
  runway after morning dew,
Bear witness to a scramble: impressions
  from flying boots of the Few.
Heinkel battled Hurricane, Messerschmitt
  via Spitfire, what contrails!
What flaming contortions, spiralling
  parachutes, oily black smoke trails.

Bob with 234 Squadron, at Leconsfield,
  endured many a frantic hour,
A trained bomber pilot transferred to an
  aquiline craft of Merlin power.
Middle Wallop, angels-high, and lots of
  'lookout for the Hun in the sun.'
Bullets, red-hot cannon shells like bats-
  from-hell, targeted by many a gun.

Bob a born aviator and a superb fighter
  ace with a strong and free spirit,
One of the Few and emerged from the
  victorious Battle with great credit.
'Down on the farm' with a Junkers 88
  painted in oils by Frank Wootton.
Bob has all the ace credentials to loosen
  and undo his tunic top button.

Victory in Europe, the ex-reporter wouldn't
  vector for London at pace,
Bob, a senior commanding officer was sent
  to the Far East victory race.
Residing in pastoral Sussex he often recalls
  his combat in the hazy blue.
Often reminisces of 1940 when it was 'Our
  Finest Hour' thanks to the Few.

The Frontline Few
Of the Battle of Britain

'Forget-me-nots where they lie'.

The esteemed 1940 fighter pilots of the
  frontline Few.
Often survival was as probable as ethereal
  morning dew.
They were young and zestful with no shortage
  of panache.
Sporty airforce blue uniforms and often a
  rolled moustache.

They defended the many by displays of bravery
  and sacrifice.
Utterly outnumbered with fatality being a toss
  of the dice.
Endless summer of nineteen-forty saw young flyers
grow tired.
As fading heavenly shooting stars their life-lights
soon expired.

Everyone recognised our aircraft of Hurricanes
  and Spitfires.
Always remember the pilots who fell on
  England's sad shires.
Pretty village churchyards and forget-me-nots
  where they lie.
Pilots in a mantle of deathly black in a clear
  pastel blue sky.

Archie McKellar D.S.O., D.F.C.* 605 Squadron.
1912 - 1940.
With thanks to Sandy Johnstone for the photograph.

Arthur Smith 1940.

Also in memory of Arthur's elder brother, Norman. He wrote an account of his brother's exploits as both boy and pilot during World War 2. Norman called his account: 'The Flyer'. I am fortunate to have lived near to Arthur and his wife, Josephine, and know that together they did such a lot to raise money for the Victoria Embankment Monument to the Few. Arthur passed away suddenly on the 22nd December 2004. Both dear friends, Josephine still, and she continues to work steadfastly for the Battle of Britain Historical Society.

The Flyer

Born 1920 at New Barnet to the Lightweight
  Boxing Champion of Europe no less.
One of three sons of whom Arthur nurtured the
  nascent skills as one might guess.
Academically bright and a star student at King
  Edward V1's Grammar School,
He naturally excelled in the ring and won all the
  trophies of the boxing pool.

Crucial health test in his final school year for the
  Anglo-Irish blood in his veins.
Lengthy fight for life against deep pleurisy and
  sharp pneumonic breathing pains.
Arthur bounced back off the ropes of death to
  qualify for the Royal Air Force,
And as a teenage pilot officer joined the 'Tiger'
  Squadron as a cub of course.

Close to death again when dive-bombed and strafed
  at Amiens Railway Station.
Fleeing from the German Army before departure
  from Cherbourg to salvation.
Returned to squadron near Hornchurch and
  exchanged danger from ground to air,
With scrambles and battles in a Spitfire to seek-out
  and destroy our enemy there.

Wingman to 'Sailor' Malan, Johnny Freeborn,
  Mungo-Park and H. Stephen.
Over the skies of Great Britain the fabulous Few
  wouldn't let Jerry brake-even.
The pivotal affair witnessed uncommon bravery
  with fiery death a twin cohort,
And yet the victory secured was far greater than
  ever hoped or sought.

Arthur was posted to other flying duties and
  promoted suitably for a test pilot.
Much progress until aircraft engines cutout and his
  survival you would not bet!
It happened one Scottish spring day in '42 and a
  canopy of trees saved his life,
Even doctors feared till Anglo-Irish blood showed
  it was not averse to strife.

Months passed and that resolute mind and body
  wouldn't give up the fight.
A boxing pedigree at stake and defeat was not
  acceptable in Arthur's sight.
No longer possessed a six feet frame but quality
  was more central than size,
Nothing to prevent our hero from negotiating other
  tasks to win first prize.

Arthur trained and taught new young airmen
  'the ropes' on how to fly.
Soon war was won and peaceful pursuits ended
  service-years in the sky.
A top osteopath who provided all of his patients
  with excellent care indeed,
And a fine boxer and fighter pilot who clearly
  inherited his father's seed.

With thanks to Josephine Smith for her kindness.

In memory of **Wing Commander Robert Stanford Tuck**
D.S.O., D.F.C. and two bars, D.F.C. (USA)

The Immortal Tuck

Bob Tuck, a gentleman oozing elegance and dignity.
Tall and slim, a sleek fighter pilot of terrific quality.
It was he, who put to waste our enemies
 of evil intent,
And despatched metal birds to their roosts hell bent.

With helmet and goggles he sat in a
 Hurricane cockpit.
Pencil-thin 'tache and a rakish scar on
 his face did sit.
Painted swastikas testify to the precision
 within his eyes,
And a camera flashed: the great Tuck immortalised.

Enigmatic and energetic, he was braver
 than the bravest.
An inspirational icon, he was quite simply the best.
Multi-coloured neckerchief typified the
 silky buccaneer,
No skull and cross-bones: mighty roundels
 to spread fear.

Tuck's biographical book is called: 'Fly for
  your Life'.
Battle of Britain and he fought on the edge
  of a knife.
An unseen hand flicked the sky-blue pages
  of his book,
Resting against the photograph of Robert
  Stanford Tuck.

Many well-informed enthusiasts regard Bob Tuck as our
finest fighter pilot.

Douglas Bader and Stanford Tuck at Hendon Museum.

The Last Goodbye

Dusk, a chilly November breeze fitfully traversed
  the North Yorkshire Moors.
Short days, an hour afore the tired sun had retired
  to lighten far-distant shores.
The aerodrome was still and the squadron of
  Lancasters sat serviced, fed and laden.
Following briefing a nervous interlude for crews
  ahead of a raid: land verboten.

An observant moon was at three-quarter and a
  few stray clouds looked down.
A night of good visibility with stars twinkling
  and navigators free from frown.
Jim piloted 'G' for George and was a veteran
  and old man at an age of twenty-two.
An Ashby-de-la-Zouch man and during peaceful
  days was happiest when he flew.

Mary was a W. A. A. F. girl and regularly drove
  the crews to their waiting giants.
Of Anglo-Flemish blood and curly flaxen hair
  and detested the enemy tyrants.
An earlier night was spent with Jim in a market
  town: not the first time but the last.
They hugged and Jim and his youthful crew
  climbed aboard and a die was cast.

The lumbering giant made speed along the
  runway and rose to join sparkling skies.
Frantic waving from cockpits and engines cried as
  ten craft faded to distant shires.
They'd said their goodbyes but Jim had a bad
  feeling on this his twentieth mission.
Children from their cosy beds heard friendly
  engines and practised their addition.

The North Sea was never welcoming and Jim
  recalled 'F' for Freddie in the drink.
Friend of the tail-gunner and washed-up at
  Cromer looking like a crumb in a sink.
They would soon be at the Baltic and then due
  south for a meet with coastal guns.
"Pilot to crew, keep a look out for Me110 fighters:
  this is where the fun begins."

The flak was fierce as they strove inland and
  shrapnel was never good company.
Jim needed to wrestle with his trusty Lancaster
  when the going got a bit bumpy.
His tail-gunner yelled as he packed tracer bullets
  into a night fighter just below.
Jim heaved the controls of his 'Lanc' and a
  corkscrew manoeuvre saved the show.

Straight and level as the teenage bomb aimer
   followed the pathfinder's flares.
Clusters of reddish-brown the night's colour until
   searchlights lit their fears.
Jim zigzagged the comb of attraction till taking a
   steady-steady straight run.
Warriors of the night rose when their packages
   were unlade and then job done!

It was at twelve thousand feet that the floor of the
   'G' for George was torn open.
Cannon shells ripped-into body of men and machine
   while in the land of verboten!
Other members of the crew died outright but Jim
   struggled on with Mary in mind,
They had been inseparable since schooldays and
   were two of a loving kind.

Lower and lower the aeroplane dropped until Jim's
   lifeblood passed a red light.
The crash was close to a Flemish village and just
   as its churchyard came into sight.
Exactly fifty years on an old lady visited the site
   and stood sadly at the cemetery.
Time had arrived for a final last goodbye as two
   souls were committed to memory.

Lancaster 'Baker 2' (ME586 UL BZ) of 576 Squadron. From rear left: Leonard Scott (rear gunner), Roy Whalley (pilot), Frederick Burgess (radio perator), Gerry McCool (mid upper gunner).
From front left: Cyril Van De Velde (flight engineer), Jack Ward (navigator), Stanley Barr (bomb aimer).
Baker 2 was shot down on 4th May 1944. Only Cyril Van De Velde (his father was from Belgium) and Jack Ward survived.
With thanks to my respected friend, Cyril, for use of his photograph.

Dedicated to **London's Defenders and Social Services during the Night War and to the memory of thousands who died during the London Blitz and 'V' Rocket attacks 1940-45**

The Night Blitz On London

Well-rehearsed wailing sirens warned the populace
  of dire invasions,
As airborne throbs announced that satanic birds
  would soon be overhead!
Men, women and children took-cover in London's
  Underground stations,
Or wearily trod to chilly Anderson shelters so
  leaving behind a cosy bed.

Searchlight batteries radiated powerful beams in
  a hunt for the intruders,
Glinting like silver sabres as they torched and
  pierced the unholy darkness.
High explosives whistled and incendiaries spiralled
  from lofty invaders,
To set the capital city aflame and turn the murky
  sky crimson in distress.

Steep-barrelled aircraft guns spat out explosive
  shells at droning demons,
And Ack-Ack burst with colours of deep red, dirty
  grey and frosty white.

Deep below in civilian shelters folk prayed and
  they numbered millions,
As firemen's machines spurted gallons of water
  onto red fires so bright!

Six story high buildings were engulfed and eagerly
  eaten by greedy flames,
Until their frail upright skeletal remains collapsed
  with a deafening roar.
St. Paul's stood proud as the conflagration raged in
  the city on the Thames,
As men of the Observation Corps noted crashing
  planes and kept the score.

Streets rang with crescendos of bells by ambulances
  staffed by God's own,
Never forgetting the hundreds killed when hospitals
  passed into eternity.
All cursed the evil crafts that murdered and sent
  many to graves unknown,
And miracles of birth as babes were born in dark
  cellars called 'maternity.'

Teddy

Teddy points the way.

Edward with his rosy-apple smile and beaming eyes
   was rarely sad.
He was something of a scruffy sight but likeable
   and a typical lad.
An intelligent boy, the first of his family to go to
   grammar school,
And he was always the fastest swimmer at the old
   quarry pool.

His dad and granddad worked manually at South Pit
   in the mines.
Back in the Thirties following your dad was usual
   for the times.
His ma was a gentle, loving soul and liked dad to
   drink his beer,
So he'd forget an awful trench war and turn his
   anguish into a tear.

Teddy passed and went to university with help from
   a scholarship.
It was around that time his poor dad died: a hero in
   a coalface slip!
They didn't find him 'cus he's buried in seams
   deep, dark and cool,
Ma went down with depression and 'ended it' in the
   old quarry pool!

Teddy left university and entered the R.A.F. to
   learn how to fly.
He swore he saw his ma's face when soaring in
   a misty blue sky.
He was a pilot when war came and fought with a
   Band of Brothers,
Everyone spoke of his bravery and sacrifice for the
   love of others.

A squadron scramble and he called 'tally-ho' over
   deepest Kent.
Ferocious was the battle where Teddy's blood was
   finally spent.
He has an epitaph on a military headstone for all
   the world to see,
Teddy the lad with the rosy-apple smile: D.S.O.
   & D.F.C.

Dedicated to **the Observer Corps and Defenders of our skies during World War Two**

The Observation Post

A balmy summer's evening enchanted by a flood
of silvery moonlight.
Jack kisses his wife, takes the tea flask and closes
the aged oak door
Of their cottage, and proceeds along the winding
lane on this 1940 night.
The moon is waxing, a ghostly-white mist hovers
over the valley floor.

He strides to the cliff-top and below wavelets
appear to roll as molten metal.
That moody lover the English Channel ripples
and sucks on the sandy beach,
And a nightingale recites sleepy notes before
deciding 'tis time to settle.
Perchance to dream of serene sunlit skies and
Berkeley Square within reach!

There's a seductive aroma from a thousand wild
blossoms on stem and bush.
Jack veers from the track and crosses a meadow
where the whispering grass
Brushes his shoes, and onto a copse of tired trees
with nesting thrush.
An irregular shadow is cast by moonlight piercing
a single opaque mass.

It is darker as he approaches a mound of sandbags
upon a hillock-high.
A capricious breeze carries the notes of familiar
voices in the cooling air,
As tiny cirrus clouds chase each other across the
starry wartime sky.
A sky pained by the deaths of pilots who perished
preserving a life we share.

The distant hum of enemy aircraft and Jack taps-out
his smouldering briar.
"One hundred plus at sixty degrees," he relays the
information to base
And awaits reply, bombers speed to London with
bellies of death and fire.
Questing searchlights like dead-men's digits reach-
out and finger wag the chase.

The vibrating aerial juggernaut passes on its
compassed northerly course.
Stained glass windows rattle as Kentish villages
endure another disturbed night
Afore the distant thud of explosives, and the
Ack-Ack's deep-barrelled voice.
An air-fleet targeted by flak and a myriad of sabre-
like torches of light.

"They're copping a packet tonight," says Jack to his
  mate sitting alongside.
Condensation rises from a cup of tea and the aroma
  of honeysuckle returns
Nature's sweet smell, striving to restore stability to
  a disturbed countryside.
Bats fly low and foxes scramble from their
  sheltering lairs as London burns!

Fewer bombers return and their paths are
  silhouetted against a vertical moon.
A twitching web alerts a spider, it races to entwine
  a fluttering hawk moth,
While a Beaufighter engages a stricken bomber
  desperate to return to its cocoon.
Jack shouts a loud approval to our fighter and emits
  a relieved nervous cough.

He looks at the far-off red-orange glow in the sky
  above the bomb-flamed city.
Dawn's first rays as Jack puffs his briar, picks up
  his flask and says farewell
To nocturnal companions, when suddenly near to
  home he is consumed by pity.
The smoking wreck of an R.A.F. aircraft with a
  charred pilot who is just a shell!

(Thinking of my mother, Pte Betty Hatter, who as an A.T.S. girl
with 602 Heavy Ack-Ack Battery was a Height and Range Finder
at Sinah Common, Hayling Island.)

The R.A.F. over Beaumanor Hall

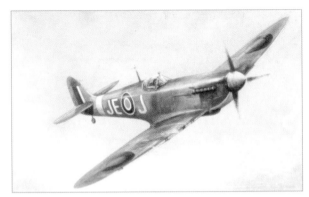

With thanks to Johnnie for the illustration.

I left home and cheerfully wandered down the
woody lane.
There's a slight gradient before it levels out to
reveal open fields.
To my right and just a minutes walk away stands
Beaumanor Hall.
It cannot be described as palatial, but it has an
aristocratic grace,
And is blessed with an abundance of character and
stately charm.
Centuries old cedar trees offer a serene, sentinel
and steadfast quality,
Representative of their age with an upstairs-
downstairs branch strata.
A classical setting offering a variety of vistas of a
manor at its best.

It once belonged to the Herrick's and one was a
distinguished poet.
A night for the Royal British Legion with music
by Holst and Rossini.
Musicians tended and tuned their instruments
under a tent-like canopy,
As natural percussions heralded the arrival of a
static-electrical storm.
The picnicking audience patiently sat on green
swards that swept afar.
Mid-summer lightning danced and darted across
the darkly sullen sky,

And thunder rumbled while moodily waiting for
Holst's dynamic Mars.
Then came the opening notes and the composer
would have been proud.

Above all of the cacophony I heard a familiar
and dynamic roar!
Contrived? Yes. But what delight to see the
concerted airborne craft.
A Spitfire akin to a silver falcon flew against
Beaumanor's backdrop.
Precious the gift of R. J. Mitchell that helped us
overcome evil's worst,
Indeed, an age when our world hovered on the
brink of self-destruction.
The sleek and elliptical-winged aeroplane gracefully
dived and soared,
And completely entranced the wonderfully
privileged audience below.
No doubt Merlin's vibrant musical had cast yet
another magical spell!

Seven times in total the slim-line legendary craft
circuited the hall.
Its wings twitched and twitched again as the pilot
signalled farewell.
A classical performance and what a finale with the
'1812' thunderclap,

As a pewter-coloured flash of lightning torched the
dim heavens above.
The Spitfire flew low over my position and I waved
with arms up high!
He had banked slightly and the pilot peered and
returned my act of joy.
There I stood transfixed until its sight and sound
was no more,
And for a few minutes all I saw was 'Station Y',
W.W.2 Code Breaker!

Beaumanor Hall, Station 'Y' during World War Two.
With thanks to the Hall for providing the photograph.

In memory of **Wing Commander F.W. 'Taffy' Higginson** 1913 - 2003

O.B.E., D.F.C., D.F.M.

Taffy in 1940.

Taffy

Taffy could only have been born in the land of song,
  Swansea, in Wales.
Entered the R.A.F. and met Tyke, George Unwin,
  a lad from the Dales.
Go-getting Taffy was a skilled fitter-air gunner but
  he sought piloting,
And showed his mettle when mastering a Gloster
  Gauntlet in training.

His treasured times were the pre-war Thirties spent
  caressing the clouds.
Cruising steamy highways and tossing gauntlets to
  earth's broken bounds.
Days of peace died when in nineteen thirty-nine
  the world fell into war,
With Taffy flying 56 Squadron Hurricanes and
  notching up quite a score.

The Battle of France and one of the Few to whom
  we are in such debt.
Awards for heroics and with a fiery Welsh blood
  held the enemy you bet!
A weighty head-on exchange of fire and a crash-
  landing alongside his foe,
With Hans Mellangrau yielding to Taffy who was
  a good boxer, you know!

The Welsh pilot officer escorted our bombers on
  vital missions over France.
He was shot down on the 17th June 1941 but led
  his captors a merry dance.
Was subject to mankind's best and worst as he
  slithered down an escape line,
Only to be captured and escape in a coal-chute
  where the sun doesn't shine.

Freedom again and trekking through dangers to
  the French southerly coast.
Picked-up by a 'Q'-ship on a mystery mission
  and onto Gibraltar for a toast.
In '43 a citation for leading his Typhoon squadron
  on sweeps over France,
Flying with supreme skill and daring that left the
  enemy with little chance.

Victory in the year '45 with flying-ace Taffy
  receiving a worthy promotion.
An officer at Bracknell until R.A.F. retirement from
  a senior staff position.
A director of British Aerospace with an O.B.E. in
  due recognition of success,
Also a respected entrepreneur with a 250-acre farm
  to administer and process.

Somewhere over a Welsh rainbow he retired to a
  life of quiet reflection.
With his dear wife, Shan and their four sons he was
  never lacking in direction.
When recalling the summer when contrails and
  smoke trials were on high,
He often spoke of his brotherly pals of the Few that
  perished in a 1940 sky.

Hurricanes of 56 Squadron.

Dedicated to **all who have flown or served with 74 Squadron**

The pilots of 74 Squadron, 1940.

Tiger Squadron

During air-battles of 1918 in the Great War came
the birth of a mighty Squadron.
Those magnificent pioneering aviators of the Royal
Flying Corps,
Welcomed the fledgling Squadron with the number
seventy-four.
Flights over trenches in Flanders and France saw
victories and a Devil's cauldron.

Names never to be forgotten like Mick Mannock,
Ira Jones, and Keith Caldwell.
Indomitable pilots who attacked the enemy with
relentless fury,
And dauntless in their SE5s with no parachutes
that's another story!
In eight months a record of 140 aircraft destroyed
plus a possible 85 boded well.

The intervening years were much to do with
continuing to develop a tradition.
In the peaceful and heavenly skies pilots learned
and mastered new skills,
And speedier single engine aircraft brought
increased power and thrills.
Young pilots sharpened lessons learnt from the
exploits of an earlier generation.

The hot summer months of 1940 provided the
ultimate test for Tiger Squadron.
They flew high-cover over the bloodstained beaches
of Dunkirk,
As Spitfires thwarted bombers intent on doing their
worst work.
Machine-guns rattled and Heinkels struggled during
a springtime's glaring sun.

R.A.F. Hornchurch and Rochford saw Tiger's
fighters roaring down a runway.
The sky was pastel blue flecked with small amounts
of steamy cover,
As pilots came, flew and perished only to be
replaced by another.
Off-duty they had a febrile excitement where
fatalistic abandon also had a play.

Memorise the names of 'Sailor' Malan, Harbourne
Stephen, and John Freeborn.
They mixed their attacks with direct head-on, beam
or from the rear,
Junkers plunged with engines ablaze and aircrew in
mortal fear.
Battle of Britain pilots called the Few treated the
invaders with anger and scorn.

From the summer month of July until the leaf fall
of October the air-war raged.
Familiar faces departed from the dispersal hut
never to return,
And Tiger cubs earned their stripes despite seeing
others burn.
They did as much as any others to secure the most
pivotal battle ever staged.

The Tiger's reputation continued to grow and grow
until it became legendary.
A valued part of the Biggin Hill Wing and led by
a superb 'Sailor',
With smash and grab rhubarbs over Europe and
never had a failure.
74 Squadron helped to destroy a wicked force and
by their deeds ensured victory.

*And the King asked Ira 'Taffy' Jones the number
of his squadron.*
*"Number 74, Tiger Squadron, the best in 1918 and
the best in the Battle of Britain".*
*The King paused, "Yes, its very good. That's Sailor
Malan's squadron isn't it?"*

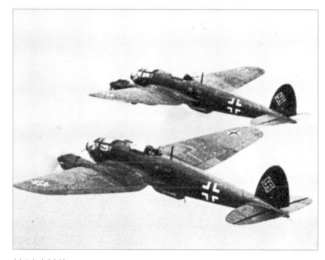

Heinkel 111's.

A Trunk Full Of Memories

A photograph in The Battle of Britain Historical Society's magazine: 'Scramble' showed letters carved in 1940 upon a tree trunk in a wood near to R.A.F. Warmwell, Dorset.

In Memory of One of the Few: Sergeant Pilot Edmond Eric Shepperd. 1917 –1940.

(152 Hyderabad Squadron)

Sulcate signs capture military memories on an
  ancient tree at Knighton Woods.
A member of '152' etched moments in time under
  a canopy of leaves and buds.
Did the day see blue skies caress salty seas or had
  bad weather stopped flight?
I wonder if the carver ever returned to his artistic
  revelry for a second sight!

Whosoever the brash artist he would certainly have
  known Edmond Shepperd.
Perhaps he refuelled a thirsty engine or cleaned the
  sergeant pilot's cockpit hood.
R.A.F. Warmwell during the Battle of Britain had
  eyes patrolling Portland Bill.
Flyers: Walter Beaumont, 'Boy' Marrs and Eddie
  Marsh registered many a kill.

So little carving yet within those deeply gouged
  letters a trunk full of memories.

An etching that links Edmond's battle in a 1940 sky
  above old Knighton's trees!
Edmond's father died of wounds sustained whilst
  fighting in the First World War.
No greater sacrifice: a son lies below a military-
  stone in Binstead Cemetery floor.

'Clouds of Fear' are always present wrote Roger
  Hall in describing aerial battles.
Every mortal fears death however bravery and
  sacrifice overcome mortal shackles.
Edmund the hero as his guns wrought destruction
  to a fighter and three bombers.
He lost his life on the 18th October 1940 and just
  missed-out on gallantry honours.

Buried on the island of his birth and neath skies
  where he fought: the Isle of Wight.
Warmwell's a calming name when autumn leaves
  turn gold and finally fall from sight.
Sulcate signs exposed to winter's frosts with spring
  and summers of dappled shade.
Seasons will never warp the honoured memories
  that are carved within a leafy glade.

Best wishes to 152 Squadron historian and friend, Danny Burt, as he continues to research the Squadron's 1940 times.

A Tale Of Human Endeavour, 1940

Pilot Officer David Harrison perished September 1940.

Their fathers fought in W.W.1 at Ypres, Arras,
  Gallipoli and the Somme.
Fought in rat infested, noxious trenches, the
  Royal Flying Corps for some.
'Over the top' and into battle in 'No Man's Land'
  or kites that fell like rain.
Letters and names, memories and brains, etchings
  on stones or church panes.

Their sons fought in W.W.2 over France, Belgium
  and England's proud shires.
Fought in Hurricanes and sleek Spitfires over
  southern counties' home fires.
'Scramble, scramble', and into battle after a
  'Tally-Ho' as kites fell like rain.
Letters and names, memories and brains, etchings
  on stone or church panes.

Their fathers fought a war, 'To end all Wars',
  winning a consummate victory.
Neatly packaged cemeteries, 'Crosses of Sacrifice',
  books intimate to history.
Trench raids and dogfights, bayonets and air war,
  diaries and logbooks to see.
A story of human endeavour, working together,
  a price must be paid to be free.

Their sons fought a war, 'The Battle of Britain',
  when stars shone in daylight.
Neatly packaged directions, 'Angels at Twenty',
  with assailants a potent sight.
Home front was a warfront: a warfront was at
  home, diaries and logbooks to see.
A story of human endeavour, working together,
  a price must be paid to be free.

The Few lay the foundations for subsequent victory.

*Their fathers fought
in the trenches.*

In memory of **Wing Commander W.B. 'Barry' Royce** D.F.C. 1913 - 1979 and **Squadron Leader Michael E.A. Royce** 1920 - 1998

Barry Royce.

Two Of The Few

One brother born afore the Great War and one soon
  after are the topics of my tale.
A six-year bridge that honoured love and respect
  for two boys from Pleasley Vale.
They enjoyed the best of times with passion for
  bicycles and anything mechanical,
And as young men they were to fight together
  against enemy hordes so tyrannical.

Typically bright and breezy and Winchester and
  Rugby Schools shared their youth.
Barry torched a pathway when learning how to fly
  whilst still young in the tooth.
He took to the lofty skies in a Avro 504N with wee
  Michael simply enthralled by it,
And as naturally as day follows night the Royce
  household had two pilots as befit.

Barry trained in business and Michael's screwdriver
  was always hot at Rolls Royce.
Just cheery weekend aviators climbing, diving and
  rolling in the cirrus by choice.
An end to the golden Thirties when tearful dark
  clouds of warfare decided to burst,
And for two young men it was 504 Squadron,
  County of Nottingham that came first.

May 1940 and the Battle of France saw terrible
  casualties including pilots of 504.
Their squadron leader and flight lieutenant 'bought
  it' so Barry took over of the tour.
Courageously the R.A.F. battled it out and destroyed
  hundreds of enemy aeroplanes,
With brothers on mark till Mike baled-out of a
  Hurricane before it burst into flames.

A brief pause in Scotland with gramophone
  melodies and ripe strawberries at Wick.
The Battle of Britain and 504 at Hendon with
  Galland and Moelders so very slick.
A fateful summer with five hundred to die in the
  defence of home skies and shores,
And oh such ability, resolve and daring deserved
  the very highest of applause.

Scramble and the pilots of 504 with their adopted
  song: 'Room 504' by Vera Lynn.
Two brothers soaring and diving in heavens of pale
  cirrus to purge the skies of sin.
Enemy bombers doing their worst by day-n-night
  over Bristol and the South West,
And after a 'cheque mate' trip to Filton we saw our
  air-knights at their very best.

Across the sea a relentless wave upon wave of
  aircraft that bombed with little pity.
The flying-boys of 504 scorched their wings and
  received the freedom of the city.
Thunderous explosions with sheets of flame,
  burning debris and smoke trails too,
With a final victory against all odds for the splendid
  young men dressed in blue!

War-years continued with Barry commanding 260
  Squadron and a veteran flyer.
Michael developed into a fine test pilot with a
  screwdriver a key part of his attire.
1945 and peace as wives and children welcomed
  two of the Few upon their return,
And may pilgrims gather at Victoria Embankment
  Memorial to pay tribute in turn.

Michael Royce.

Barry Royce at Dispersal, 1940.

Sandy Johnstone, 1940.

Sandy

Born in Glasgow during the Great War, just afore
  the Battle of the Somme.
I remember Sandy as a charming gentleman, a fine
  and heroic Scotland son.
At an eager eighteen years he took to the air with
  602: 'City of Glasgow.'
Squadron fuselage code: 'LO' soon had the enemy
  praying 'goodbye' below.

In 1939 Scottish Spitfires from Drem intercepted
  bombers raiding Scapa Flow.
Eliminated many of intruders around the Firth of
  Forth in a scintillating show!
1940 and Sandy's guns ravaged a Heinkel 111
  and Junkers 88 just east of Dunbar.
Fierce engagements in England's southern shires
  with the battlefront extending far.

A Battle of Britain squadron leader who led from
  the front and always by example.
Cared deeply for the men in his charge and by
  measure of courage possessed ample.
An ace pilot with a variety of victims, double
  figures when all's taken into account.
He flew with some of the greats, Archie McKellar,
  Bob Boyd and Micky Mount.

On 1st October 1940 received a Distinguished
  Flying Cross for inspiring headship.
In early '41 he was posted to the Middle East and
  the first of many a foreign trip.
Alexander Vallance Riddell Johnstone was a
  Group Captain by the end of the war.
In early 1951 he undertook the posting of station
  commander at Ballykelly for sure!

Seconded to Malaysia to form the Malaysian
  Air Force, then returned to England.
A final promotion to Air-Vice-Marshal and
  doubled-up, Air Officer to Scotland.
When the sun's embers were fading after a round
  of golf on a verdant sword of green,
Sandy would look to the heavens and recall long
  lost friends or was it all a dream.

Sandy Johnstone front centre with 602 Squadron at Westhampnett 1940. Sandy's pal and my old friend, Paddy Barthropp, is on the back row third in from the right. With thanks to Sandy for the photograph.

Dedicated to **Wing Commander C.F. 'Bunny' Currant** 1913 - 2006
D.S.O., D.F.C.,* Croix de Guerre, Mentioned in Despatches*

And recalling his great friend Pilot Officer I. J. 'Jock' Muirhead. D.F.C. (K. I. A. 15th October 1940)

With Halo and Wings

It was indeed God's blue heaven in the late Thirties:
the pre-war days.
Wispy cirrus with cumulus, nimbus and all their
kaleidoscopic ways.
Two daring young pilots with solar haloes and fixed
wings on aircraft,
Took to soaring-n-diving with assistance from a
rotary propeller shaft.
Gloster Gauntlets that danced and pranced in a
heavenly iridescence.
A glorious time of many decades ago and now
drifting to evanescence.

1939, World War 2 and many cities subject to aerial
enemy bombing.
Civilians suffer black tear-laden clouds and death
with folk-a-sobbing.
Two intrepid young pilots named Bunny and Jock
of 605 Squadron.
Fighter pilots of the brilliant Few who defied the
devil's cauldron.

They defended our homeland and the future of our
daughters and sons.
Heinkels, Messerschmitts and Junkers fell to the
twosome's guns.

Bunny crash-landed and Jock tested the risky merits
of a parachute.
He insisted that a caterpillar badge was preferable
to the direct route.
1940 and huge air fleets a source of constant
pressure by the Luftwaffe.
Hundreds in air-armadas that packed the sky and
the Few did suffer.
Dear Jock was gravely outnumbered, badly strafed
and he bought it!
The Scot traded in his solar halo and acquired one
of heavenly fit.

"Jock was a lion with wings, a brother", said a
desolate Bunny.
Brave and dependable and with an outlook that
was endearingly sunny.
We remember squadron pals: 'Widge' Gleed and
Archie McKellar.
Both were regarded as finest of the brave - bravest
of the fine to a fella.
1941 and Bunny took command of 501 Squadron
and a bit-part actor too.
David Niven a good friend and starred in the film:
'First of the Few'.

Bunny on a swoop in his Spitfire SD-Z and badly
  shot up over France.
Bullet in his skull and F.W.190's intent on giving
  no second chance.
A resolute struggle to Lympne Airfield and aircraft
  does a cartwheel.
He is strapped into cockpit and upside down, life
  can seem so surreal.
"The sweet smell of cut grass and the drip, drip of
  fuel onto hot metal."
"Distant ring of fire-engine strangely reminds one
  of a boiling kettle!"

1942, the esteemed Wing Commander C.F. Currant
  led a Wing at Ibsley.
A precious and memorable moment: marriage to
  Cynthia, a dear fiancée.
Commanded 122 Wing when Europe was stormed
  on the 6th of June 1944.
Bunny so focussed and calmly in control for
  whatever came in store.
Undoubtedly a highly decorated fighter ace, sincere,
  brave and glorious.
It is little wonder that in God's blue heaven the
  R.A.F. were victorious

(A very dear and respected friend)

From left: Flying Officer David Fulford, Bunny Currant
and Leslie Howard in 'First Of The Few'

*"Bunny will always fly high,
especially in a heavenly sky!"*

A pre-war photograph taken by Bunny whilst piloting a Gloster Gauntlet.

Conclusion

John Dundas in 1940.

The contents within this book have been written from the deepest depths of my heart. I believe and hope that Battle of Britain enthusiasts, military historians and poets will warmly applaud my efforts. To me what is equally important is to help the uninitiated to understand and appreciate the debt that we owe to the pilots of The FEW.

Before closing, I must draw readers' attention as to how Great Britain lost the services of some of her most brilliant sons. I take for example, John Charles Dundas of 609 Squadron. He was educated at Stowe School and at the age of seventeen won a scholarship to Oxford. John gained a first in Modern History at Christ College, and won an award that took him to the Sorbonne and Heidelberg.

During his service career he accounted for nearly twenty aircraft, the last being on 28th November 1940 that of top German ace, Major Helmut Wick. Almost immediately Wick's number 2 caught Flying Officer John Dundas D.F.C. in his sights, and John plunged into the sea. A Channel bed was to be his final resting place, but how post-war Britain could have used the services of such brilliant young men! The Battle of Britain was without doubt the most pivotal battle ever fought for the reasons mentioned in my introduction, and victory was brought about by a magnificent combined effort. The book is not intended to present a crème-de-la-crème of the Few; it simply contains a selection of my work. It is true that many of their names are well-known and ace pilots, but all of their number played an important role. Many 'wingmen', those who covered the tails of more senior pilots, received tremendous acclaim and decorations for sacrifice and exceptional bravery.

I am delighted to write that in September 2005 Prince Charles unveiled a 'Memorial to The Few' on the Victoria Embankment, London. Dame Vera Lynn was there, also. It is utterly unbelievable that it has taken sixty-five years for such a monument to appear in our capital city, especially as a great chunks of the air-war was fought there. I cannot thank the government for a cash injection nor the Lottery, even though they were asked to contribute. Our gratitude must go to a group of individuals from the 'Battle of Britain Historical Society.' I am proud to be a member, and know personally the nucleus of individuals who have 'worked their socks off' to achieve their objective. Amongst many other concerns they have arranged fund raising events and attracted a handful of famous celebrities who have donated large sums towards the millions of pounds that were required. In addition, The Daily Mail has been brilliant in several activities and the Society is truly grateful.

Michael Kendrick

A donation from the sale of every book will be made towards the future maintenance of the Monument.